THE ENCYCLOPEDIA OF

SEWING TECHNIQUES

A step-by-step visual directory, with an
inspirational gallery of finished works

Wendy Gardiner

RUNNING PRESS
PHILADELPHIA, PENNSYLVANIA

Vogue ® Patterns For Living 1596 by Susanna Stratton-Norris

A QUARTO BOOK
Copyright © 2003 Quarto Inc.

All rights reserved under the Pan-American
and International Copyright Convention.

First published in the United States in 2003
by Running Press Book Publishers.

9 8 7 6 5 4 3 2 1

Digit on the right indicates the number of this printing.

Library of Congress Cataloging-in-Publication Number 2003100660

ISBN 0-7624-1651-3

Conceived, designed, and produced by

Quarto Publishing plc
The Old Brewery
6 Blundell Street
London N7 9BH

QUAR.ESET

Project editor **Kate Tuckett**
Art editor **Karla Jennings**
Assistant art director **Penny Cobb**
Designers **Michelle Cannatella, Karin Skänberg**
Copy editor **Sue Richardson**
Photographers **Colin Bowling, Paul Forrester**
Illustrators **Kate Simunek, Kuo Kang Chen**
Proofreader **Jenny van Heerden**
Indexer **Jonathan Burd**

Art director **Moira Clinch**
Publisher **Piers Spence**

Manufactured by Universal Graphics Pte Ltd., Singapore
Printed by Midas Printing International Ltd., China

This book may be ordered by mail from the publisher.
Please include $2.50 for postage and handling. But try your bookstore first!

Running Press Book Publishers
125 South Twenty-second Street
Philadelphia, Pennsylvania 19103-4399
Visit us on the web!
www.runningpress.com

CONTENTS

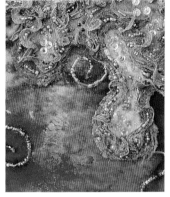

INTRODUCTION

Sewing is such a huge subject and with today's modern equipment, almost all types of sewing—from straightforward dressmaking and soft furnishings to exquisite embroideries and creative "painting with thread"—can be stitched easily by machine.

In this *Encyclopedia of Sewing Techniques* I have tried to cover most of the everyday sewing techniques, as well as provide some guidance on many of the creative sewing disciplines, using and choosing fabrics, interfacings, tools and notions.

Before starting to sew, choosing and using the right tools for the job makes every sewing project much easier to complete. Thus the few chapters cover all the essential basic equipment, sewing machines, what to look for and useful functions, as well as tips on choosing and using fabrics and reading and properly understanding paper patterns.

Having mastered all the basic equipment, our dictionary of common stitches and sewing terms provides a handy reference guide. Armed with this listing, you can confidently tackle any projects found in books, magazines or paper patterns and know what you are talking about!

In addition to the basic sewing terms and stitches, we've included all the essential up-to-date techniques for both hand and machine sewing including basting, hemming, buttonholes, zippers, darts, gathers and ruffles, fitting collars, cuffs, waistbands, and facings. We've also covered some easy tailoring and couture sewing techniques. Combine these with the in-depth, step-by-step instructions for sewing a whole host of different seams, applying trims and appliqué, modern top stitching ideas and working with today's glorious range of specialist fabrics and you really are ready to go and sew!

An encyclopedia would not be complete if it didn't cover many of the new innovative techniques to help make sewing fun and easy so we have a whole section on some of the different creative sewing methods with which you can embellish, decorate or furnish. Try your hand at patchwork and quilting, trapunto or stumpwork. Learn to sew and cut fabric for a chenille effect, mola and reverse appliqué, or delicate cutwork. Use stabilizers, not just to support stitching, but to shape exquisite sculptures and have hours of fun with free-motion embroidery.

Finally, if you are short of ideas, take a look at our inspirational Gallery in which we share the creativity of many skilled sewers. Ideas range from straightforward dressmaking to artfully creative manipulation of fabric and embroidery by machine.

I've had great fun writing this book and hope you thoroughly enjoy it and find it an invaluable companion as you tackle many varied sewing projects in the future.

Gardiner

Wendy Gardiner

chapter one

SEWING BASICS

Tools and materials
Choosing and using a sewing machine
Choosing and using fabrics
Using paper patterns
Common stitches and sewing terms

TOOLS AND MATERIALS

Having the right tools for the task in hand can make all the difference to the ease, speed, and finishing results of a project.

NEEDLES

These can be split into hand and machine needles. There are a huge variety of needles for both disciplines, each slightly different to suit different jobs.

Hand needles

Whether you wish to repair a hem, hand stitch some embroidery, cover sofas, or repair soft furnishings, there is a needle to suit. The length of the needle and the point shape and size depends on the needle type. For instance, when sewing leather, a needle with a triangular cutting point is ideal, whereas tapestry needles are blunt with rounded tips. ◄

Mixed household needles A pack of mixed needles is handy to have. It will include large-eyed needles for heavyweight threads and fine needles for light work. As with all needles and pins, replace them regularly as blunt needles can snag fabrics. ▲

Self-threading needles These have a split eye at the top and are ideal for the partially sighted.

Ballpoint needles With rounded tips, these are used to sew jerseys or stretch knit fabrics as they part rather than pierce the fibers.

Beading needles Very fine, and sometimes curved, these have a small flat eye so that the whole needle will slip through small beads with ease.

Darning needles With a large eye, these are designed to cope with thicker threads, and have a rounded, fairly blunt tip.

Soft-furnishing needles

Coming in a range of sizes, some of these needles are curved so that you can take the needle from front to back and out to the front again in one motion—ideal when finishing sofa or chair covers where it is not possible to get to the reverse of the item.

Crewel needles These have a large eye to accommodate thicker threads, and are usually used for embroidery.

Bodkins These needle-like tools used to thread elastic or ribbons through casings. Generally flat with a large eye, they are available in different lengths. ►

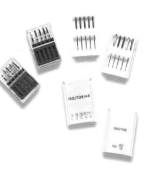

There are also other specialist needles including extra long doll needles, leather-point needles, curved upholstery needles, carpet needles with large eyes and blunt tips, and long weaving needles.

> **TIP** *Cut thread end at an angle for easy threading.*

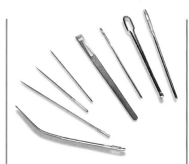

Hand-sewing needles are sized and shaped to suit different tasks. Some are curved, some have large eyes for thick threads, others have very fine eyes for beading. Bodkins look like large-eyed needles and are used to thread tape, ribbon, or elastic through casings.

Machine needles

Having the right sewing machine needle helps you stitch evenly, and prevents snags, unwanted gathering or visible needle holes, etc.

Machine needles have a flattened shank on one side, which is used to ensure the correct insertion of the needle. Generally the flat part is faced to the back of the machine (check your user manual). If the needle is incorrectly inserted it may move about or stitches may be skipped. ▶

Keep a pack of mixed-size universal needles in the workbox—use smaller, fine needles with lightweight fabrics and larger, thicker needles with heavy fabrics.

Which size? Generally, if the needle breaks when stitching (without any apparent justification), it may be too small—try a larger size. If the seam pulls up or stitches are skipped, the needle may be too big, try a smaller size. American sizes range from 9–20 and European sizes 60–120. Needle packs are usually numbered with American/European sizing— the larger the number, the larger/stronger the needle. ▲

In addition to general-purpose needles, there is a whole host of needles with different size and shape tips to sew denim, stretch fabrics, machine embroidery, or leathers.

Universal/multi-purpose These are ideal for most woven fabrics, synthetics, and knits. The size of needle needed will depend on the weight/ thickness of fabric being stitched. The heavier the fabric, the larger the needle size required.

Ballpoint With rounded tips that part rather than pierce the fabric fibers, these are used for jersey, stretch knits, velvets, and fleeces.

Stretch These needles have a specially designed "scarf" to help stitch two-way stretch fabrics such as lingerie or swimwear fabrics, those with Lycra™, or rubber. Using this specialist needle will help prevent skipped stitches.

Jeans Although these are called jeans needles they are suitable for any type of dense fabric such as canvas, upholstery fabric, and of course denim. They have a sharp needle, often with a blue top. They are also excellent for top stitching on heavier fabrics or for sewing faux suede.

Leather This has a chisel point to help penetrate real leather.

Sharps These are also known as microfiber needles, and have sharp tips. They are ideal for sewing silks, microfiber fabrics, and densely woven fabrics, for top stitching, and sewing buttonholes.

Embroidery Machine embroidery, which generally requires a highly concentrated amount of stitching, needs a special needle. These needles have larger eyes, sometimes with a specialist coating useful when stitching specialty threads such as metallics and rayons, which can otherwise wear away a small nick in the eye of the needle.

Twin One shank, two needles, which will stitch two parallel rows of stitching in one pass. Great for decorative heirloom stitching, or top stitching, the gap between the needles can vary from approximately $\frac{1}{16}$–$\frac{1}{8}$ in (2–3mm). Twin needles are also available as ballpoint, universal, stretch, and embroidery needles. ▼

Wing These are specialist heirloom needles that are designed to leave little needle holes in the fabric as they stitch.

Quilting These generally have a longer, sharper point, so they will pierce layers of cotton and batting easily whilst maintaining a straight stitch. ▼

Spring needle This has a spring wrapped around the needle shaft. It is used for free-motion embroidery. ▼

Sergers (overlockers) Sergers need different needles and again, these are available in a choice of sizes and finishes to suit different fabric types. Check your serger manual for details of which needles to use and when.

TIP Use a fresh needle for every new project.

WEIGHTS AND PINS

Weights and pins are used to temporarily anchor two or more layers of fabric together, or to hold pattern tissue in place whilst cutting out.

Weights are ideal when working with large, flat pieces, such as curtains. Pins are used on smaller, shaped areas that require more stability. Look for pins made of hardened and tempered steel that are virtually rustproof.

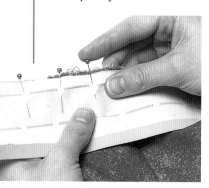

Pins

There are a number of different types of pins—short, thick pins for handicrafts, long, fine pins for bridal work, and a whole host of sizes and types in between.

Dressmaking pins Usually made from hardened and tempered steel, they come in different lengths. ▶

Glass- or plastic-headed pins General-purpose pins, these have colorful bobble heads that make them easy to remove and see if dropped. Glass-headed pins will resist the heat of the iron. Avoid pressing over plastic-headed pins as the head will melt. ▶

Sequin and bead pins These are short, flat-headed pins used to hold sequins or beads in place. ▼

Ballpoint pins Like ballpoint needles, these have a slightly rounded tip and are used on stretch-knit fabrics.

Bridal and lace pins Long and fine, these are specially made for fine bridal fabric and laces.

Corsage and craft pins These are also long, with a large glass or plastic head. ▲

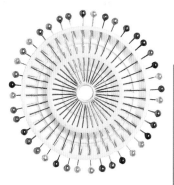

Quilting pins These can be glass-headed or flat-headed but are usually extra long, enabling them to hold several layers of fabric together. ▲

Loose-cover pins These may be double-pointed or have spiral twist shanks and are used to hold loose covers in place.

Safety pins These have a covered end in which the sharp pin is enclosed and held. Safety pins are available in different sizes and shapes, including badge pins, dress-shield pins, diaper pins, kilt pins, and stitch-holder pins. ▲

As with needles, replace pins that become blunt with use as they can snag fabrics.

When pinning tissue to fabric, place pins along the seam line, parallel to the cutting line.

When pinning fabrics together, pin at right angles to the seam so the pins can be removed as you stitch. ▼

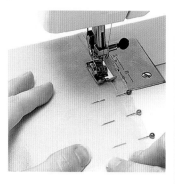

Pin baste fabrics by pinning at regular intervals. On light- to medium-weight woven fabrics, pin every 3–4 in (8–10cm). On heavier weight fabrics pin every 5–6 in (13–15cm). On fine, slippery fabrics pin every 2–3 in (5–8cm). Also pin more frequently at curves or sections that are being fitted together, such as sleeves, gathered waist to waistband, etc.

Weights Special sewing weights have drop-down pins in the bottom that anchor onto the fabric, keeping them in place. As an alternative to these weights, use food cans (check the can is clean before placing on fabric).

THREADS

Thread was originally made from natural fibers only—cotton, linen, or silk. Nowadays, these fibers are mixed with nylon, polyester, rayon, or viscose to produce strong, economical, and versatile threads with different combinations being suitable for different types of fabric.

Which thread? With the huge range of threads available today, deciding which to use and when can cause confusion. As a general rule therefore, select a thread with a similar fiber content to the fabric being sewn. Thus, use 100% silk with silk fabric, 100% polyester with polyester fabric, or 100% cotton with a wool crêpe.

A good, all-round thread type is a polyester-covered cotton. This has the strength of cotton with the flexibility of polyester. It is ideal for general-purpose sewing and dressmaking. This type of thread is also good for knit fabrics as it has more elasticity and will "give" as the seam in the garment stretches.

Silk threads These are ideal for sewing by hand as they are soft and gentle to handle. They also provide a high luster to the stitching. However, silk thread is more expensive than general-purpose thread, so use for top stitching or hand stitching.

Metallic threads These are generally used for decorative stitching either by hand or machine. If sewing on a machine, use with a machine-embroidery needle, as the metallic fibers in the thread can cut a minute groove in the eye of the needle, which may then cause the thread to shred or break. ▼

Metallic threads add a shimmer and shine and can make simple stitching a beautiful decorative feature.

Machine embroidery Again, usually a high-gloss thread, machine embroidery thread is of a slightly finer gauge than general-purpose thread as it is often stitched in a highly dense pattern. This type of thread comes in a huge variety of colors and can also be metallic, variegated, or iridescent. It is usually 100% cotton or a mix of cotton/polyester. ▼

TIP *If the metallic thread is uneven or bulky, use it on the bobbin rather than threading through the top. Sew with the project face down so when turned over, the specialist thread is on the right side.*

Bobbin fill This is a fine thread, usually available in black or white, used in the bobbin when stitching machine embroidery. As it is finer, it reduces the bulk of thread in concentrated areas of stitching and helps produce a soft, even stitch.

Quilting 100% cotton or a polyester/cotton mix, quilting thread has a wax finish to prevent tangling when hand or machine stitching.

Basting A finer thread, usually 100% cotton, that will break easily but should not tangle or knot when hand basting.

Top stitch A thicker, sturdy thread, usually polyester, this thread is used for top stitching, sewing on buttons, or for decorative sewing. Use a regular thread in the bobbin.

Transparent/invisible This is a nylon thread, available in smoke or clear colors only, and is designed for hand or machine use, for repairs, quilting, and attaching trims.

> **TIP** *Use a machine-embroidery needle to prevent splitting or breaking threads.*

Serging/overlocking threads
Sergers use lots of thread through the loopers and needles that combine to form the seam and overcast stitches and thus there are special serging threads, which are fine and strong and come on larger reels (bobbins) and cones. ▲

100% spun polyester/cotton-wrapped polyester Similar to conventional sewing thread

but finer, these threads are available on large cones of 1000 yards (1000m) or more. This type of thread is used in the needles.

Woolly nylon/floss This has a woolly or flossy texture and should be used in the upper loopers. It is recommended for lingerie, swimwear, or fabrics with Lycra™, and provides a shiny, decorative finish. A similar type of thread is a bulk thread, which gives a matte finish and is good for stretch or knitted fabrics as it gives good coverage on knitted edges.

Decorative threads
Conventional decorative threads can be used in the loopers, which have larger-eyed needles.

> **TIP** *Rather than re-thread the machine each time a thread is changed, cut the old thread near the spool and tie on the new thread. Pull the old thread through at needle until the knot is reached. Cut off the knot and thread new thread through the needle.*

> **TIP** *To color-match thread to fabric, unravel a length of thread and hold it against the fabric, as it will lighten slightly off the reel. If a perfect match is not available, select a shade darker.*

Decorative hand sewing
As with general threads, there are lots of different types of decorative threads for hand sewing, cross stitch, embroidery, crewel work, etc. Threads may be 100% cotton, a mix of fibers to give strength, gloss or sheen, and come on skeins, in braids, or on spools.

Embroidery floss/stranded cotton These threads are made up from a number of strands. These are separated and used in combinations of 1–3 strands at a time, depending on the thickness of the thread desired. ▲

Perle or mercerized crochet thread This is 100% cotton and has a sheen. It can be used for crochet, or for cross stitch or other embroidery.

> **TIP** *Use good-quality threads for all sewing projects, and avoid using cheaper brands as they are often made from uneven fibers that result in uneven, rough thread, which is easily broken.*

CUTTING TOOLS
Nowadays, a good pair of scissors for sewing is just part of the tool kit. Today, there are various sizes and shapes of scissors for a range of different sewing tasks.

Shears
Dressmaker's shears are the most important cutting tool for a sewer. They are different from scissors as they have molded handles, with a smaller hole for the thumb and a larger one for the fingers, and are shaped for either right- or left-handed use. The blades are long and straight so that a smooth cut is possible. Often the handles are at an angle to the blades so that the blades can sit parallel to the cutting surface, ensuring the fabric remains flat.

Serrated blades

Very fine serrated edges on the cutting edge of the blades hold slippery fabrics in place as you cut. Ideal for fine fabrics, silks, satins, etc. ▲

TIP *Keep the blades working smoothly by lubricating the screw area occasionally with a tiny drop of machine oil. Wipe the blades on kitchen paper before using again to prevent oil getting onto fabric.*

Scissors

Scissors have handles with the same size and shape hole for fingers and thumb, thus the same pair can be used either right- or left-handed. ▲

Soft-grip handles

Look for scissors with soft-grip handles that are easier to use for prolonged cutting. Also available are scissors with handles one on top of the other designed to be used in one hand. They have a spring action to open the blades between each cut. ▲

Pinking shears

Again, these shears have shaped handles and are thus designed for right- or left-handed use. The blades have a definite zigzag cutting edge that provides the "pinked" cut used to neaten the raw edges on seams. Particularly useful for cottons and other non-fray fabrics or craft projects. ▲

Needlework or embroidery scissors

Keep a small pair of short-bladed scissors to hand. The small size provides greater control for cutting intricate areas or around notches, and clipping and snipping. ▼

Machine-embroidery scissors

Similar to normal embroidery scissors, the difference is the curve of the blades at the tip end. They are used to snip threads very close to the work, particularly when machine embroidery is held taut in a hoop.

There are other specialist scissors designed for specific tasks, such as appliqué scissors, which have a shield to hold the fabric flat as you cut, and buttonhole scissors, adjustable to cut specific buttonholes. ▼

CUTTING ACCESSORIES

Sharpeners

Keep your scissors and shears sharp for a longer life by running them through a scissor sharpener. These sharpeners are also designed to remove burrs and nicks. However, they cannot be used with serrated-blade scissors.

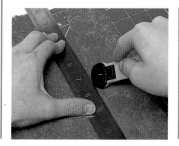

Rotary cutters and mats

Rotary cutters are ideal for cutting long lengths of fabric for soft furnishings, or for cutting bias strips and patchwork fabrics. Some have retractable blades or changeable blades for different cutting effects. They are used in conjunction with a cutting mat and ruler and can cut several layers in one sweep.

Seam ripper A quick unpick or seam ripper is usually supplied as part of the sewing-machine tool kit. It has a curved bladed end, usually with a bead on the top arm of the blade. They are used to unpick incorrectly stitched seams by slipping the blade under the stitch and slicing through. Repeat along the seam every 1–2 in (25mm–5cm) before gently pulling the seam apart. They are also ideal for cutting open buttonholes. ▶

MARKING TOOLS

Markings are used to transfer placement lines, darts, etc., from pattern tissue to fabric or to make sure left and right, front and back match so that a good fit can be achieved with accuracy. Traditional tailor's tacks can be used (see Basting, page 46) or a variety of marking pens and chalks available.

Chalk markers Using a chalk marker is a quick method of marking and can be easily brushed

away once used. However, in order to transfer the markings from the tissue to the fabric, the tissue has to be cut carefully first to allow the chalk to be used on the fabric.

Chalk markers come in many shapes and colors—including the traditional tailor's triangle of chalk, chalk wheels, chalk pencils with plastic brush on the end, and chalk blocks.

Chalk wheels When pushed along the placement line, working in only one direction, these leave a very fine trail of powder. They are ideal for marking long lines, such as pleat lines, buttonhole placements, and hemlines. ▲

Chalk triangles/blocks Similar to the wheels, these can be used in any direction and leave a heavier chalk line. ▼

Chalk pencils Depending on the markings required, these can be used in the same way as ordinary pencil-marking lines, crosses, dots, etc. Use a color that contrasts with the fabric and mark on the wrong side.

To mark darts

1 Snip away the tissue from marking dots, then make placement mark on the top layer of fabric.

2 Place a pin right through fabric layers at this point, then turn the layers over and mark the reverse piece at the pin point. Repeat for all placement points.

Marker pens

Pens are a quick and easy alternative to chalk pencils. There are different types available, from water soluble to fadeaway or permanent.

TIP Avoid marker pens when working with dry-clean-only, or very lightweight fabrics where the pen may bleed through.

TIP Markings are usually made on the wrong side of the fabric. However, it is still a good idea to have a range of marking tools to hand in order to suit the tool to the fabric being marked.

Water-soluble pens These are usually blue and the mark is removed later, using a damp sponge or by washing the garment. ▼

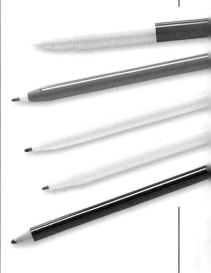

Fadeaway/vanishing pens/pencils The marks literally fade away after a limited period (usually about 48 hours). These are sometimes called evaporating or air-soluble pens. ▲

Dressmaker's carbon paper and tracing wheel

Also known as dressmaker's tracing paper, this is used to trace markings on two layers of fabric at the same time. Suitable for light- or medium-weight fabric, it is advisable to mark the wrong side of the fabric, as indeed with all marking methods.

1 Temporarily remove pattern tissue and re-fold fabric pieces so that the wrong sides are together.

2 Slip a piece of folded carbon paper between the layers, with the carbon toward the fabric. Re-pin tissue paper in position.

TIP *Use carbon paper that is only a slight difference in color from the fabric.*

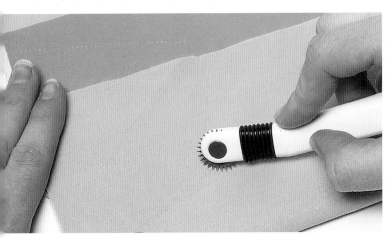

3 Using a tracing wheel and a ruler as a guide, run the wheel over the markings to be transferred. ▼

PRESSING

Pressing techniques

Pressing is different from ironing in that the iron is pressed down, moved only slightly before being lifted, and replaced further along. With ironing, the iron is moved back and forth to remove creases.

- Press each seam before it is sewn over again. If possible press each seam as it is sewn.

- Preferably press from the wrong side or, when pressing the right side, use a press cloth.

- Test a fabric remnant before steaming the main fabric to see how it reacts to steam and heat.

TIP *Pressing with a hot iron can set even vanishing or carbon markings, so always test them on a scrap of the same fabric before marking the main fabric.*

Essential pressing equipment

One of the key elements to successful sewing is to press repeatedly. To do this, a few pressing aids are essential.

Steam iron Choose a steam iron with different functions—from light spraying to surges of full steam.

Press cloth This can be a square of self fabric, a lightweight cotton, or transparent organza. Using a press cloth, you can press at a hotter temperature.

TIP *Choose a cloth that is transparent so you can also see the area being pressed.*

Seam roll This stuffed sausage shape is used to press long straight seams in small areas—such as sleeves. An alternative is a tightly rolled towel. ▶

Ham/tailor's ham This is a oval, well-stuffed "ham" shape used to press curved areas such as darts and princess seams. ▼

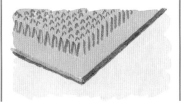

Needle/velvet board This is a board of fine needles, which is used to press pile fabrics such as velvet, fleece, or corduroy. The pile is placed face down so that the pressing action doesn't crush it. An alternative is a soft, fluffy towel. ▼

SEWING MACHINES AND SERGERS

Today's sewing machine make sewing a breeze—they are easy to use and help you produce professional-looking results, whatever fabric you use.

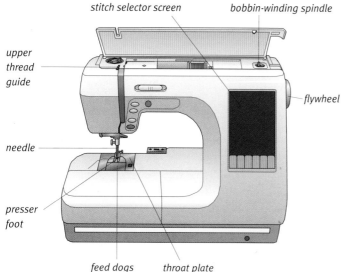

stitch selector screen

bobbin-winding spindle

upper thread guide

flywheel

needle

presser foot

feed dogs throat plate

Using a sewing machine speeds up the process of sewing considerably, as well as ensuring neat, secure seams. A machine can also produce evenly stitched buttonholes by memorizing and repeating the same size time and again. It can help apply zippers in minutes. As well as all this, you can stitch decoratively for added finishing touches.

Modern machines are designed to make sewing simpler. Even very basic machines have a choice of stitches built in, plus a selection of presser feet to suit different stitch techniques. The computerized models also automatically set the stitch length and width to suit the fabric being stitched, advise on presser foot for each application, and have LCD touch—screens enabling you to easily alter stitch type, length, width, etc. It is very difficult to get the tension wrong as they have such great tolerance and they are capable of stitching anything from a single layer of fine fabric through to multi-layers of heavyweight fabrics. With all machines, the tension is correct when the top thread shows on the top of the fabric and the bobbin thread shows on the bottom. The threads interlock between the layers.

SEWING MACHINE TERMINOLOGY

The appearance of each sewing machine differs slightly, depending on the manufacturer, level of machine model, etc. However, the general principles are the same on all (check your user manual for positioning and access of the relevant features).

Thread spindle/spool pin
Each machine has one or two. The second is used when stitching with a twin needle (which has two needles on one shank). The way the thread should come off the reel (up and over, or under and up) will depend on the model. It is important to place the reel on the spool the correct way, as it affects the stitching (check your user manual).

Thread tension guide This controls the upper thread and helps form stitches correctly— the average tension setting is often marked on the guide. ▲

Bobbin-winding spindle
Again, the direction in which to thread the bobbin will differ with each machine—check the user manual for threading guidelines. Some machines can have bobbins wound without unthreading the top thread. Do check that the needle disengages when

bobbin winding—if it doesn't do this automatically, disconnect it by pulling the button on the flywheel.

Flywheel (also known as a balance wheel) Located on the right end of the machine, this can be turned to lower and raise the needle one step at a time. Older models may also have an inner disk that is pulled out to disengage the needle when bobbin winding. ▲

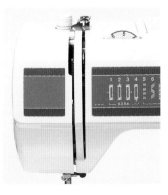

Upper thread guides The way to thread the machine correctly is often marked and numbered on the machine. If not, check your user manual and follow the procedure as directed. ▲

Needle The needle has a flat section on the shank. On most machines this is placed facing the back of the machine. The needle is held in position by a screw or a lever held in place by a screw. Most machines have a choice of needle positions, center, right, and left. ▼

Presser foot The presser foot helps to keep the fabric flat and guide it through the feed dogs. Different presser feet are used for different applications, for instance, a zipper foot cuts away sections so the stitches can be made close to zipper teeth. A beading foot or appliqué foot will have grooves in the base so it slips easily over concentrated stitching. On most machines a lever lowers and raises the presser foot. On modern machines, presser feet snap on, making them very easy to remove and replace. ▼

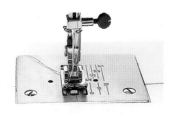

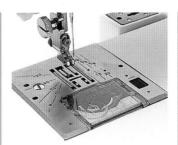

Feed dogs These raised jagged edges move back and forth to guide fabric through as it is stitched. On most modern machines the feed dogs can be lowered so the fabric can be moved in any direction as you free-motion embroider. ▲

Throat plate (or needle plate) This fits over the feed dogs and usually has markings to indicate different width seam allowance distances from needle position. The needle goes down through the throat plate opening to meet the bobbin thread and form the stitches. Some machines provide an alternative, smaller-holed throat plate to use when sewing delicate lightweight fabrics that may be pulled into the hole otherwise. ▲

Bobbin case and bobbins The wound bobbin is either placed straight into a drop-in bobbin case, or slipped into a bobbin holder and inserted vertically into a rotary-hook case. The drop-in bobbins are very easy to use, particularly for those with arthritic fingers. The bobbin area needs to be cleaned frequently using the little brush provided in the sewing-machine toolbox. Failure to clean out fluff regularly can cause the machine to jam. ▼

Free arm This is the term used to describe the narrowed base achieved when the flat-bed extension is slipped off. It makes sewing small areas such as cuffs, pant hems, etc. much easier as the item can slip on to the free arm. ▼

Stitch selection All machines have a choice of utility or built-in stitches, which can be chosen by turning a dial or combination of dials or pressing buttons, or touching an LCD display screen. These are basic stitches used in general sewing and include straight stitch, zigzag stitch, stretch stitch, blind hem stitch, etc. To use these for different sewing techniques, the length and width can be altered, thus, for example, a zigzag stitch can be used to overcast a raw edge or as a tight satin stitch for buttonholes or appliqué.

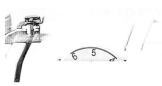

Computerized machines will also set an optimum length and width of stitch but can be overridden to achieve the desired effect.

Stitch length The length of each stitch can be chosen by turning a dial or button, or touching an LCD screen, in the same manner as stitch selection. There will be a minimum and maximum stitch length. On some machines the stitch length is marked in millimeters, on others by number of stitches per inch (check your user manual to determine which method your machine uses). The length of stitch required will depend on the bulkiness of the fabrics being sewn together. As a general rule, the finer the fabric, the smaller the stitch required, and the thicker the fabric; the more numerous the number of layers being sewn together, the longer the stitches need to be.

STITCH LENGTH GUIDE

Very lightweight chiffon/voiles/muslins—set stitch length between 10–12 spi (stitches per inch) or 2–2.5mm
Lightweight cottons, polycottons, georgettes, etc. (used for most general sewing)—set stitch length between 8–10 spi or 2.5–3mm
Medium-weight gabardine, wools, worsteds—set stitch length between 7–9 spi or 3–3.5mm.
Heavyweight wools, fleeces, tweeds, meltons, etc.—set stitch length between 5–8 spi or 3.5–6mm (depending on number of layers being sewn together).

The stitch length will need adjusting for other sewing techniques also—lengthen to longest stitch for machine basting, slightly increase for ease stitching, decrease at curves and corners to reinforce the area.

Stitch width This is applicable when stitching sideways stitches such as zigzag or decorative stitches. The width can be increased or decreased to suit the stitch and fabric choice in the same manner as stitch length.

THREADING GUIDE

Upper thread Although all machines are threaded slightly differently, the basics are the

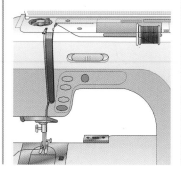

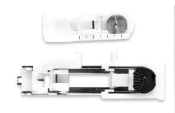

same. The thread comes off the reel, which is held on the spool by a retainer. It goes through a guide on top of the machine, which holds it in place, then down and up through tension disks before being looped over a hook on the needle lifter (always thread with needle raised as far as possible), then down to be threaded through the needle from front to back. Incorrectly threading the upper thread can be a major cause of thread breakage, skipped stitches, or too tight stitches. Follow the user manual diagram carefully.

Bobbins Wind the bobbin winder so the bobbin thread is wound evenly and at a constant tension. If the bobbin is too loosely or unevenly wound it may jam. (Sometimes it is desirable to wind specialist or thick threads on the bobbin by hand. When this is the case, stitch slowly.)

Most machines come with several empty bobbins and, although you can buy universal bobbins, generally try and use those supplied with the machine. For general sewing, use the same thread in both the needle and bobbin. When using specialist threads as the upper thread, use a general-purpose or bobbin-fill thread in the bobbin and vice versa if using thicker thread in the bobbin.

The bobbin is threaded around the bobbin case as indicated in the user manual. To bring up the bobbin thread, turn the flywheel slowly to lower the needle, which will catch the bobbin thread. As the upper thread comes back up, pull it gently from the back to bring up the bobbin thread loop. Pull both together a short way.

PRESSER FEET

Using the right foot for the application makes sewing easier and more accurate. Every machine comes with a range of sewing machine feet for the basic sewing functions, including a general-purpose foot, zipper foot, embroidery or appliqué foot, blind-hem foot, and buttonhole foot.

General-purpose foot Used for straight stitching, this foot has two equal-length toes and an oblong gap through which the needle goes.

Zipper foot This is used to insert zippers and is shaped to allow stitching close to zipper teeth. This foot may have a central toe either side of which the needle can penetrate, or a choice of snap-on positions to move the foot from side to side.

Embroidery/appliqué/satin stitch foot Often made of see-through plastic, this foot will have a high, wide groove on the underside to help it glide over decorative stitching.

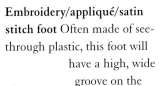

Blind-hem foot This foot usually has a wide toe to the left, with a guide and a narrow toe to the right. The guide is used to guide the folded edge of the fabric.

Buttonhole foot Most modern machines have special feet for buttonholes. Some will measure the button and automatically stitch the correct size hole. The underside of this foot has deeper grooves to allow it to glide over satin stitching.

Overcasting foot This foot is specially designed to stitch at the edge of the fabric. The wire brushes on the bottom prevent the fabric edge from puckering or rolling.

Walking foot This is a special, bulky looking attachment that is used for hard-to-feed fabrics. This foot prevents the fabric layers from separating and "walking." It is great for pile fabrics, matching plaids, or quilting through several layers.

WHEN PROBLEMS OCCUR

As the machine stitches, fluff builds up in the bobbin area. If not cleaned regularly, this can cause bobbin jams. Every machine comes with a cleaning brush in its equipment package. Remove bobbin and de-fluff regularly.

If the top thread reel keeps bouncing up and down the spindle, the thread can tangle or break. Prevent this happening by adding a reel restrainer to the spindle, keeping the thread in place. One or two are usually supplied with the machine.

> **TIP** *It is rarely necessary to alter tensions on modern machines and a small alteration to tighten or loosen the tension goes a long way, so adjust very slowly, a little at a time.*

Lubrication Most modern machines are self-lubricating and thus do not need oiling. However, check the user manual and oil as indicated.

Skipped stitches These can be caused by incorrect threading. Also, make sure that the needle you are using isn't blunt or incorrectly inserted.

If the problem persists, try a finer needle. However, if the thread keeps breaking, try a thicker needle.

Tension As well as altering the length of the stitch to suit the fabric, it is occasionally necessary to alter the tension. Together, the correct tension and stitch length form even stitches, where only the top thread shows on the top and only the bobbin thread shows on the underside. To adjust the tension, refer to your manual.

BUYING A SEWING MACHINE

There are a huge variety of machines with prices ranging from hundreds of dollars to thousands. The choice can only be one of personal

> **TIP** *Test drive different machines using your own fabric samples to see which handles them best.*

preference. However, there are a few basic features that are essential for easy sewing.

* A machine that easily sews all fabrics—from fine voiles and chiffons to heavy brocades, velvets, or layers of denim. Most modern machines have a variable foot pressure, that can easily stitch different weights.

* Variable stitch speed, allowing you to control the speed of sewing—slower at tricky areas, curves, or corners and faster when sewing long, straight seams.

* Snap-on feet that are easily removed and replaced. Make sure of a good basic selection.

* Easy threading of bobbin and needle. Can the bobbin be wound without unthreading needle? A useful feature when thread runs out mid-seam. Drop-in bobbins are less fiddly than rotary-hook bobbins—ideal for arthritic fingers.

* A large aperture and wide flatbed are preferable when sewing large items. Some machines have an optional extra extension table available.

* Look for extended guarantees when purchasing.

* If you need to carry your sewing machine around, check the weight and carrying case for portability.

* Are there additional accessories or can you update your computerized machine easily? As with all advanced technology, new models with upgraded specs are constantly being introduced.

> **TIP** *Always buy a sewing machine that can do more than you think you need so that you will not outgrow it.*

USING AND CHOOSING SERGERS

A serger (or overlocker) is another type of sewing machine that stitches seams, trims excess seam allowances, and neatens raw edges, doing so extremely quickly. It may use 3–8 threads depending on the model. The stitches are flexible, are created very quickly and provide a professional finish.

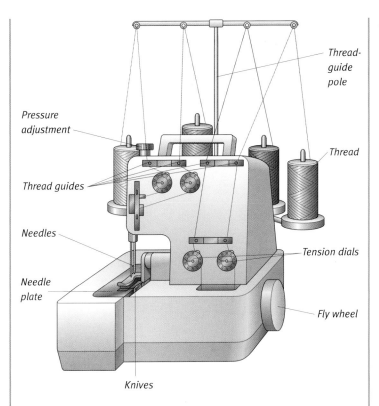

Pressure adjustment

Thread guides

Needles

Needle plate

Thread-guide pole

Thread

Tension dials

Fly wheel

Knives

The stitches are formed by needle threads combined with upper and lower loopers. Each of these has its own thread tension, which is adjusted to create different stitch effects.

A serger uses far more thread than a conventional sewing machine and thus the thread is usually finer and comes on cones or large bobbins.

A serger stitches in a different way to a conventional sewing machine and thus has different elements.

Loopers These take the place of bobbins. The looper threads come up from underneath the needle plate and are called the lower upper looper threads.

Needle threads The number of needle threads will depend on the type of serger—if it is a three-thread machine it has a one-needle thread, and so on. The fewer the number of threads, the smaller the range of stitches that can be formed. Sometimes only 2–3 threads are required for a flat seam—in this case the other needles can be disengaged.

As well as stitching and neatening seams, sergers can overcast seams stitched on a conventional machine, produce a flat lock stitch that can be used for decorative outside seaming, or to do blind hemming, lettuce hemming, and narrow hemming. Some machines can be used to add faggoting or chain stitch. A serger can also use decorative threads in the loopers, which have larger-eyed needles. This may also necessitate deactivating the cutting knives.

Starting to stitch

1 Test the stitching on a sample of fabric before working on the main garment.

2 Start with the presser foot down or up and serge 2–4 in (5–10cm) of chain stitch before introducing the fabric.

3 Hold this thread chain to the back and feed the fabric under the foot so that the seam allowance will be trimmed.

Finishing a seam

1 At the end of the seam, continue stitching for 5–6 in (12.5–15cm).

2 Secure the thread tail and stop unraveling by threading it onto a large-eyed needle and inserting back through the overcast edge.

Stitching with a serger

Below are some examples of how you can stitch on a serger.

Flat lock

Two-thread overlock stitch

Chain stitch

Blind hem

Narrow hem

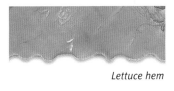

Lettuce hem

Sample of decorative stitching, knife off

CHOOSING AND USING FABRICS

The right choice of fabric, cut and stitched correctly, can make all the difference to the outcome of a project. Here is a list of common fabric types, together with some tips on how to sew and press for best results.

COTTONS AND LINENS

These are stable, woven fabrics that are easy to sew, thus ideal for beginners. Both cotton and linen are natural fabrics but both are often mixed with synthetic fibers for added strength, crease-resistance, etc. Cotton comes from the cotton plant, while linen comes from flax. They can range from light- to heavyweight and can be used for dressmaking, crafts, and soft furnishings, depending on the weight and type. Interfacings can be fusible or sew-in— of a weight to suit the fabric. Use general-purpose thread and neaten seams

Cottons and linens

with overcasting, zigzag stitch, or pinking shears. These fabrics can be pressed with a hot iron.

Broadcloth Traditionally made of cotton, other fibers are now also used. It is a light, tightly woven fabric with a soft, slightly napped surface.

Broiderie anglais (eyelet embroidery) Again traditionally a cotton fabric, it has self-colored embroidered holes as a decorative finish.

Calico An inexpensive cotton fabric, plainly woven with a smooth finish. Different weights are available for dressmaking and soft furnishing use. Calico is often used to make a *tulle* (a sample garment on which to check fit, etc.).

Chambray Traditionally cotton, it is sometimes mixed with other fibers, with the warp woven in white. Similar in appearance to denim although lighter.

Cheesecloth A loosely woven cotton fabric, used for crafts or for lightweight fashion items.

Chintz A closely woven cotton fabric that has a glazed finish. Often used in crafts and soft furnishings, and usually printed in bright colors.

Cottons, polyester/cotton Lightweight, suitable for craft projects and summer clothing, cotton fabrics are easy to sew, come in a huge variety of colors and designs, and are easily laundered.

Cotton batiste A very lightweight, soft, sheer fabric. Bastiste can also be made in wool or synthetic fibers.

Corduroy Traditionally made in cotton, nowadays other fibers are used. It is a corded fabric with a woven or sheared rib that has a velvet-like nap.

Damask Usually used for table linen and home furnishings, damask is made from linen or cotton on a jacquard loom

(the warp and weft are matte and shiny, producing a self pattern).

Denim A medium to heavyweight twill-weave fabric that is hard wearing. The colored warp and white weft is very distinctive. Nowadays denim is available in a variety of colors as well as blue.

Denim

Dobby/piqué Less elaborate than a jacquard weave, this has a small pattern incorporated into the weave.

Drill, canvas Heavier-weight cottons for outdoor or hardwearing items. Drill has a strong twill weave. Canvas is also used for interfacings.

Egyptian cotton and cotton lawn These are lightweight cottons with specific uses. Egyptian cotton makes wonderful sheeting, while cotton lawn is crisp but lightweight and is most often used for heirloom stitching, christening gowns, or for lining bridal wear.

Gauze A very lightweight sheer fabric, usually made of cotton or silk.

Gingham A two-tone check fabric that can be used for dressmaking or crafts.

Linen, handkerchief linen, and linen-like fabrics A distinctive feature of linen fabrics is that they crease very easily. Treat them in the same manner as cottons. Handkerchief linen is very lightweight.

Gingham

Muslin This is a plain-weave fabric that is usually lightweight and used for interfacings or crafts.

Poplin Woven with a fine horizontal rib, poplin is slightly heavier and crisper than cotton lawn.

Sail cloth A very firmly woven cotton canvas used for sails.

Sateen This is a strong, lustrous fabric usually made from cotton. The spelling of the name differentiates it from satin.

Seersucker This fabric has a permanently puckered or crinkled effect made up of alternating stripes.

Voile A very lightweight, sheer, plain-weave fabric. Used in home furnishings for lightweight drapes, it can also be used for summer wraps.

Voile

Vogue ® Patterns For Living 1596 by Susanna Stratton-Norris

SILKY FABRICS

These include silks, satins, crêpe de chines, polyester, viscose, and rayon. They can range from light- to heavyweight and are used for all manners of dressmaking. Sew-in and fusible interfacings are suitable. Seam neatening is necessary as they usually ravel. Either overcast or bind seam allowances with tricot tape. Iron on a silk setting and use a press cloth.

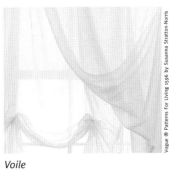
Silky fabrics

Acetate A chemically made fiber that can be added to other fabrics to give a silky finish. A great background fabric for machine embroidery, it can be dissolved with acetone to give a lace-like finish.

Acrylic Another synthetic fiber that is often added to other fabrics to bring warmth to the fabric.

Brocade A luxurious heavyweight fabric that usually incorporates a jacquard design of flowers and leaves. Used for evening wear.

Chiffon A sheer, light fabric that drapes—originally made of pure silk but today often of man-made fibers. Chiffon is used for wraps, as over-blouses or skirts.

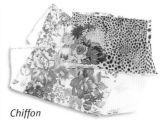
Chiffon

China silk Usually a lining silk fabric, it is lightweight with a plain weave. It is also known as jap silk.

Ciré A lightweight fabric with an extremely slippery and shiny finish.

Crêpe-backed satin This can be used either side as it is a double faced fabric, also known as satin-backed crêpe. It is often used for bridal wear and evening wear.

Crêpe de chine Traditionally a pure silk, lightweight fabric, it is often made in man-made fibers today, making it more versatile and hardwearing.

Doupion This is a double fiber fabric woven from two fibers of silk from silkworms cocooned together. It has a thick, uneven texture. Synthetic doupions are also available and are less expensive. Silk doupion makes lovely tops and lightweight jackets.

Doupion silk

Faille This has a narrow rib, which gives it a slightly heavier finish than crêpe de chine. Traditionally silk, faille is also made in other fibers today.

Georgette Similar to chiffon, georgette is also sheer but made with crêpe yarns so it has a slightly more opaque finish.

Nylon A man-made fiber that provides toughness and durability when mixed with other fibers.

Organdie/organza Another lightweight, sheer fabric, but slightly crisper than chiffon. Often made in polyester.

Ottoman Like faille, ottoman has a crosswise rib, only this is slightly wider. Also made in wool and man-made fibers.

Peau de soie Traditionally made from pure silk, this is now made in polyester also. It has a soft luster and is slightly heavy in weight. Ideal for evening wear and bridal gowns. The polyester version is often known as peau.

Polyester, viscose, rayon, polyester crêpe de chine These man-made fabrics mimic the handle and look of natural fibers but are often cheaper to buy and easier to sew. They will ravel easily so do need to be neatened well. Use lightweight interfacing, either sew-in or fusible, to match the handle of the fabric.

Polyester, viscose and rayon

Silk noil, raw silk These are silk fabrics with a raw or nubbed surface texture and shading. Treat as a pile fabric and use "with nap" layout.

Satin, satin-backed crêpe and duchesse satin A high-sheen fabric, satin is medium weight and ideal for evening wear. Use "with nap" layout to ensure even shading. Satin-backed crêpe can be used with either side as the right side and is ideal for evening suits. Duchesse satin has a highly lustrous sheen on the right side and is widely used in bridal wear.

Shantung Traditionally a plain-weave silk fabric with occasional slubs for textural interest, it is now made in polyesters also.

Taffeta, paper taffeta and moiré taffeta Originally a plain-weave fabric and made from silk, taffeta has a crisp finish and shiny surface. Paper taffeta is lightweight and very crisp, while moiré has a watermark finish and is usually luxurious and crisp.

Thai silk As the name suggests this comes from Thailand. It is heavily slubbed, often brightly colored or iridescent.

Tulle Traditionally used for bridal veils, tulle used to be made from a fine net of silk. Nowadays it is often also made from nylon or other man-made fibers.

Tulle

WOOLEN/FLEECE FABRICS

Nowadays there is a great variety of woolens ranging from lightweight to heavy meltons and tweeds. Lightweight woolens can be used for blouses and dresses, while the heavier weight types are used for coats and jackets. If the fabric has a sheen, such as cashmere, use "with nap" layouts. Press, preferably from the wrong side.

Wool, fleece and gabardine

Alpaca, angora Both are wool fabrics used for luxury items. Alpaca comes from the llama and is a soft, silky, lightweight cloth. Angora is woven from the angora goat hair, also making a soft, silky fabric. It

is often woven with other fibers to produce a woolen cloth for coatings.

Barathea This is a traditional fabric, originally made from a silk and wool mixture. It is very smooth with a broken rib pattern.

Bouclé This is the term used to describe a thick, stubbly surface texture. Bouclés can be knitted or woven and usually have a dull, textural surface. Ideal for jackets, vests, etc.

Camel hair Another luxury fiber woven from the under hair of

Bouclé

a camel, this is usually mixed with sheep's wool to combine luxury with durability. It is usually left undyed and is distinguished by its soft yellow color.

Crêpe, challis These are lighter-weight fabrics with a crinkled surface created by being woven with a crêpe yarn. They can be used for general dressmaking, are easy to sew and have minimum stretch if pattern pieces are placed on grain lines. Fusible or sew-in interfacing is suitable.

Cashmere, melton, and mohair Use the "with nap" layouts. Test press a scrap first —use a fluffy towel as surface if necessary. Trim pile from seam allowances or reduce bulk by grading the seam allowances. Use a lining fabric for facings to reduce bulk also.

Fleece A fabulous fabric that is easy to work with, comes in many colors and designs, doesn't need neatening, washes easily, and can be used for many outerwear garments and accessories, or soft furnishings. However, press with care as hot irons leave marks. Use a seam allowance that is slightly larger than usual to help feed fabric layers evenly and then trim close to stitching to reduce bulk in seams.

Fleece

Felt This is made from a mix of wool and other fibers, rolled and pressed together to produce a tightly finished flat surface. Felt is mainly used in crafts and millinery.

Flannel This has a soft, brushed appearance and is often used for pants or suits. Flannelette is a lightweight fabric, usually made from cotton, and is often used for children's nightwear.

Gabardine Gabardine has a close twill weave and is a strong fabric, ideal for suits, jackets, pants, or lightweight coats.

Herringbone Traditionally made in wool, this has a reversed twill weave, creating the effect of a backbone of herring. It is used mainly for coats and suitings.

Gabardine

Loden Similar to duffel cloth, it is a thick, heavy, napped fabric used for coats.

Melton Another densely woven fabric with a slight nap and a very smooth appearance. It is used for coats and uniforms.

Mohair Also made from angora goat hair, mohair can either be used alone or mixed with other fibers for suitings and coats.

Nun's veiling A plain-weave, sheer fabric, literally used for nuns' habits.

Serge Traditionally a hardwearing suiting fabric, this has a twill weave.

Tweed-Harris, Irish, Scottish, Donegal A tweed is traditionally woven from wool with colored slubs of yarn giving it a shaded, textured surface that is also sometimes slightly hairy. Donegal tweed was originally woven in County Donegal in Ireland, while Harris tweed is still only woven in the one place, Harris in Scotland. Tweeds are normally heavyweight and they may have a nap and directional weave, therefore use "with nap" layout. Use lining fabric for facings to reduce bulk. Neaten seams with overcasting.

Tweed

Vicuna One of the most expensive and luxurious of wools, it is woven from the hair of a llama. Hard to dye, it is usually used in its natural color of brown.

Worsted This is the term used to describe the way the yarns are carded and combed to eliminate short fibers, thus producing a smooth surface. Woolens are only carded and are not as durable.

Fur, fake fur, faux fur Fur fabrics can have a long shaggy pile, be close cut, or be somewhere in between. Fake furs do not ravel so do not need neatening. Reduce bulk in the seams by trimming away fur pile from seam allowances. Finish seams by using a sturdy pin andpick out the fur along the seams to cover and disguise the seams.

Fake fur

TIP *If fabric sticks as it is fed through and a specialist foot is unavailable, try sprinkling talcum powder on the fabric along the stitching line.*

Synthetic leather/suedes

These include faux suede, ultra suede, suedette, leatherette, and leather. These rarely need neatening so seam allowances can be trimmed close to stitching. Reduce bulk by grading the seam allowance—trimming one just ⅛ in (3mm) and the other ¼ in (6mm). Use weights or tape when cutting and if pins are needed, ensure they are only used in the seam allowance as they may make holes in the fabric. If presser foot sticks to leather, use a roller foot or teflon-coated foot.

Synthetic leather and suede

Velvet—panne, chiffon, velveteen, sculptured, and devoré

Velvets are luxury pile fabrics that can be man-made, cotton, or silk. They can be floaty and lightweight, or heavyweight. A devoré velvet has parts of the pile burned away to leave a raised pattern. All velvet has a definite shading and can be difficult to sew because the piles

Velvet

rub together, causing them to "walk" when stitching seams. Avoid this by double pin basting and thread basting and using a walking foot. Make sure all garment pieces are cut with nap running in same direction. Decrease bulk in seams by grading seam allowances. Neaten seams with overcasting or binding with tricot tape.

STRETCH FABRICS

Fabrics that have stretch need to be sewn in a way that allows them to continue to stretch. This includes using zigzag or stretch stitches, woven interfacings, and ballpoint needles. Prevent excessive stretching at armholes, neck edges, etc. by stabilizing with edge tape, and press with care, using a press cloth. Take care when pinning as snags and runs are easily caused by catching with pins.

Stretch fabrics

Chenille This is a pile yarn with either a knitted or a woven finish that has a fuzzy or novelty texture.

Cotton knits Usually a fine gauge fabric, cotton knits are extensively used in fashion and sportswear. They are often mixed with other fibers for greater durability and to lessen shrinkage.

Double knit This is a firm knitted fabric that is very stable. It looks the same on both sides and has a fine lengthwise rib.

Jersey Originally this was a knit fabric with purl stitches on the right side and plain stitches on the reverse. However, nowadays, many other lightweight, soft knitted fabrics are given the same name.

Lamé, Lycra™ and spandex These are specialist fabrics used for dancewear or swimwear. Lamé contains a mixture of metallic yarns and can be woven or knitted. Lycra™ is the trade name for a two-way stretch fabric that is tightly woven and comes in many different colors.

Stretch velour Similar to velvet this has a tightly woven short cut pile. Polyester velours are used for leisure and sportswear.

CUTTING-OUT TIPS

Probably the most important element to consider when cutting out fabric is to match grainlines. The lengthwise grainline, which is the one most commonly referred to, runs parallel to the selvages (the bound side edges of fabric). Below are a few tips on working with grainlines. For other cutting-out terms and techniques, turn to Common stitches and sewing terms, page 32.

Lengthwise or straight grain
This runs parallel to the selvages and has the least stretch. Place pattern pieces on the fabric so the marked grain lines (bold line on tissue) are completely parallel

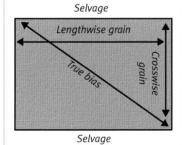

Selvage

Lengthwise grain

True bias

Crosswise grain

Selvage

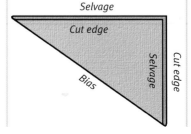

Selvage

Cut edge

Bias

Selvage

Cut edge

with selvage. Fabric cut off grain will have more "give" and stretch.

Crosswise grain

This is at right angles to the lengthwise grain and follows the threads that run from selvage to selvage. There is slightly more give or stretch in the crosswise grain. Some pattern pieces can be cut on the crosswise grain. Simply mark the new grain line on tissue, by marking it at right angles to that printed, and then match new grainline to selvage as before.

Bias and true bias

Bias is any diagonal direction. True bias is at a 45-degree angle to lengthwise grain and is found by folding fabric so that lengthwise and crosswise grains meet. Fabric cut on the bias is at its most stretchy. Garment sections cut on the bias may need stay stitching or edge stitching at curved areas such as necklines.

Matching plaids and checks

Only use checks or plaids if the paper pattern suggests them in the "suggested" fabrics. Cut out with care as follows:

1 Cut each piece from a single layer so that the tissue pieces can be placed with care on fabric.

2 Make sure the stripes and checks are squared off and that wide stripes or checks do not run across the widest part of the pattern piece (that is, the bust or hips).

3 When cutting second pattern piece, match up balance marks and notches so that the pattern continues unbroken across seamed pieces. ▼

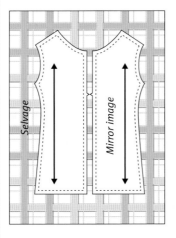

Selvage

Mirror image

SEWING WITH SPECIALIST FABRICS

Specialist fabrics often have special finishes applied, or may be embroidered or beaded. They require special treatment. Follow the "with nap" layouts, use sharp scissors to cut the fabric, and change needles frequently as they will blunt more easily. Use sew-in interfacings and press with care, always with a press cloth.

Taffeta, chiffon, georgette, organza, and voiles Fabrics that shimmer and gently change color through the width or length of the piece are called iridescent, ombre, or changeant (changeable).

When cutting out make sure balance marks and notches are in line across fabric so color variance matches. Use lots of pins to secure flimsy fabric and sharp serrated-edge shears.

Sequined/beaded fabric These are luxury fabrics, often used as part of a garment. Remove beading and sequins from seam allowances by carefully cutting away or crushing.

Choose simple designs for highly beaded or sequined fabrics. Cut on a single layer of fabric, turning pattern pieces over to ensure right and left sides. Use the "with nap"

> **TIP** When handling cut beaded fabrics, apply drafting tape to stop sequins or beads unraveling on cut edges.

> **TIP** If the beads are bulky and cause stitching problems, try using a zipper foot.

Specialist fabrics

layout to cut all pieces in the same direction. Use sew-in interfacings or a layer of matching lining fabric when sewing transparent fabrics.

Fabrics with surface detail— pre-pleated, ruched, crushed, etc. Do not press fabrics with pre-pressed surface detail. These include crushed velvets, and crinkled and pre-pleated fabrics. Trim seam allowances and bind with tricot tape. Make sure you match balance marks and notches with same surface detail on both sides.

Surface detail

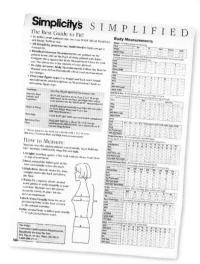

USING PAPER PATTERNS

Commercial paper patterns are available for all types of sewing, from dressmaking and costumes to soft furnishings and crafts. Most of the pattern companies follow an international sizing code as well as using similar pattern markings and terminology.

Pattern contents

The contents of a pattern envelope include a printed tissue with all pattern pieces to make the items shown on the envelope front, and a step-by-step instruction sheet for cutting out and construction. Many patterns are now multi-size so that there are cutting lines for a range of sizes around each pattern piece.

Also included on the envelope will be line drawings/ illustrations showing details such as pocket placement, zippers, type of waistband, etc., as well as suggested fabrics, notions required, and measurements for each size included in the design.

Fabric requirements

The amount of fabric to make each item is listed, including a "with nap" or "without nap" requirement. The choice of suitable fabrics includes those in which the pattern has been tried. Only use plaids, checks, or stripes if they are listed.

Pattern sizing

The size of pattern you require is not necessarily the same as your ready-to-wear size, thus take accurate bust, waist, and hip measurements before choosing the pattern. All commercial pattern catalogs have a measurement chart in the back with which to compare your measurements and their sizing. You may also find you are a different size for top and bottom.

> **TIP** Use your bust measurement to choose the best patterns for tops, jackets, and dresses. Use your hip measurement for pants or skirts.

The basic measurements needed to determine pattern size are:

Bust Around the fullest part of the bust. Tape to remain parallel to the floor.

Waist To find the natural waistline, tie a string around the waist and bend side to side.

It will roll into the crease that forms at the natural waistline.

Hips At the fullest part—approximately 9 in (23cm) below waist.

Pattern type

Patterns are also sized for different body types. An average woman is categorized as "Misses" and is 5'5"–5'6" (165–168cm) with a B cup size. Larger, more mature figures are categorized as "Women or Women Plus" while teenagers have "Junior/Teen" sizes. Children's patterns are sized by age and average measurements.

Fit and ease allowance guidelines

All patterns have an allowance for "fit or wearing ease" and may also have a "designer" ease. The amount contributes to the finished size and whether the garment is meant to be close or loose fitting.

The wearing ease is the amount of "wriggle" room added, thus a close-fitting bodice will have very little, while a coat will have enough to enable it to be worn over a jacket. The designer ease is the fashion ease, the extra fullness the designer builds in to create the silhouette required.

As a guideline, the following allowances are frequently used:
Knit-fit Very close (garment measures at or under body measurement).
Close fit Very close, ¼–½ in (3–6mm) ease.
Fitted Garment contours closely to body.
Semi-fitted Garments skim the figure, following body shape.
Relaxed/loose fit An "easy" fit with 5½–7 in (14–18cm) allowance for tops or 4–5½ in (10–14cm) for skirts and pants.
Very loose fit Best described as oversized, this type of garment is very loosely fitted with ample room inside.

TIP *Compare the finished-garment measurements printed on the pattern envelope or pattern tissue with your body measurements to see the difference in size and amount of ease allowed.*

Pattern markings and notches

More helpful information is printed on each of the pattern tissue pieces, including the number of pieces to cut, how to lay them on the fabric, and any placement marks for buttonholes, darts, or pockets that need to be transferred.

Multi-size Several sizes are marked on each piece. Sometimes the cutting lines of the different sizes are indicated by a different type of line—dotted, dot and dash, or plain. The advantage of multi-size patterns is that you can cut from one size to another (say, a size 14 top to 12 hip).

Although the seam allowance is included in most commercial patterns it will not be shown on the tissue of multi-size patterns because the number of lines needed would be confusing. On average, dressmaking patterns have ⅝ in (15mm) seam allowance. Other types of pattern have ¼ in (6mm).

Notches The pattern piece will also have notches—triangular marks in the cutting line. These are used to match corresponding pieces, on sleeves/armholes, collars/neck edge, or facings/front edge.

Circular markings Used to indicate placement darts, pockets, zippers, facings, etc.

Grain line This is particularly important as pieces cut off-grain will not hang properly and may sag or bag later. The straight grain of the fabric runs parallel with the selvage edge of the fabric (bound side edges). The grain line on the tissue is shown by a thick, straight line. The tissue pieces need to be positioned so the tissue grain line runs completely parallel with the fabric grain line.

Fold line Some pattern pieces can be placed on the fold of fabric, cutting two symmetrical halves at once.

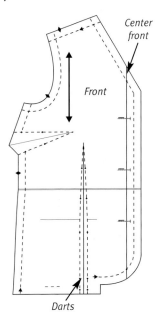

Center front

Front

Darts

TIP *Highlight the layout you are following when putting tissue onto fabric to ensure you keep to the same one.*

Place the fold line against the fold of fabric (with fabric folded so selvages match).

Lengthening/shortening line To alter the length of a pattern piece, it needs to be cut at a point that will not affect the style. Patterns that can be altered have a lengthening and shortening line.

Tucks, pleats, and buttonhole placement These are shown by dotted or dashed lines. Pleats and tucks may also have directional arrows between the lines, indicating which way to fold the fabric to form the pleat.

Fabric layouts

Each of the items included in the pack has a fabric-layout guide, usually two or three depending on the choice of fabric widths that can be used or whether the fabric is "with nap" or not. The layout includes all the pattern pieces needed with an illustration of how to lay them on the fabric. It will also indicate whether to cut from single or double layers of fabric.

COMMON STICHES AND SEWING TERMS

There are many different stitches used when making up garments or soft furnishings that make seams stronger and prevent them from stretching when they shouldn't, or that hold facings and linings in place. There are also many sewing terms, frequently used in commercial patterns, magazine projects, or craft books that aim to help you—as long as you know what they mean.

COMMON STITCHES

Understanding terminology is the first step to sewing with confidence, so this chapter brings together a directory of frequently-used sewing terms to help you acquaint yourself with the language of stitch. Refer to it as you sew, or use it as a quick reference guide, so that the next time you read or hear of, say, notches or basting, you'll know what they are!

Straight stitch

This is the most basic stitch used to join two or more layers of fabric together. The stitch length required depends on the thickness of fabric and number of layers to be sewn together. A good average length to start with is 2.5mm, equal to about 10 stitches per inch. However, always test on a sample of the same fabric/ number of layers before working on a project. Increase the stitch length for bulky fabrics. If the stitch length is too small it will start to pucker the seam. If it is too big, it will appear loose and gather easily.

When stitching round corners, slightly decrease the stitch length for a neater finish.

Ease stitch

This stitch is used to join a slightly longer piece of fabric to a shorter one, for example, sleeve heads to sleeves. It is similar to gathering, but there should not be any visible folds or creases on the outside of the garment once the seam is stitched and pressed. ▼

1 Loosen the needle tension slightly and increase the stitch length to between 3 and 5mm (about 5–9 stitches per in). The actual stitch length used will depend on the bulkiness of fabric—thicker fabrics require longer stitches.

2 Stitch within the seam allowance, close to the seam line. On commercial patterns you will have markings showing where to ease stitch. Alternatively, stitch areas that will be curved, stitching approximately ½ in (13mm) beyond area. ▲

Back stitching

This is simply a straight stitch that goes backward and is used to secure stitching at the beginning and end of a seam.

Most machines have a button or lever to hold whilst stitching, allowing you to stitch in reverse. (Check your user manual for your particular machine's method.)

• Hold the thread tails (this will prevent them being pulled into the bobbin case or tangling) and, starting 1 in (25mm) from the end, stitch a few stitches backward and then start going forward to end of seam. Repeat at the other end.

Stay stitch

This stitch is used to prevent curved or bias-cut edges such as necklines or shoulders from stretching out of shape as you handle them. ▼

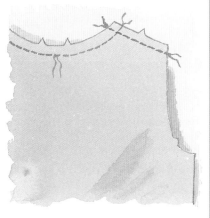

1 Use a regular stitch length and machine approximately ½ in (13mm) from the raw edge.

2 To prevent the fabric stretching as you stay stitch, stitch in the same direction as the fabric grain. To determine this, "stroke the cat," running your finger along the cut edge. The fibers will curl smoothly in one direction, just as a cat's fur does. Stitch in this direction.

TIP *Overcast the seam edges on all garment pieces before joining and stitching the seams together.*

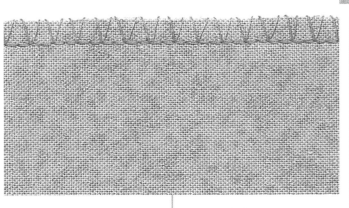

Overcast stitch

Overcast stitch or overlocking is the stitch used to prevent the fabric raveling. It is stitched on the very edge of the trimmed seam allowance. ▲

1 On a conventional sewing machine, select an overcast stitch or choose a zigzag stitch. For lightweight fabrics select a smaller stitch width. For heavier fabrics choose a larger stitch length and width.

2 Stitch with the right side of the stitch just overlapping the edge of the fabric. ▲

Under stitch

This is a regular straight stitch used to prevent the inside layers of fabric, such as facings, from rolling to the outside.

1 Trim seam allowances, grading and clipping as required (see pages 84–85).

2 Open out facing and press the seam allowances toward it.

3 On the right side of the item, stitch a scant ⅛ in (3mm) from the seam line, through the facing and seam allowance only.

4 Press, then turn facing to inside. Press again.

Edge stitch

This is an extra row of stitching on the right side of the fabric. It is similar to top stitching (see below) but is usually much closer to the fold, seam, or finished edge, and is usually stitched in matching thread. If you are a beginner or unsure of your stitching accuracy, leave it out. ▼

1 Press edges to be stitched.

2 Use a zipper foot or clear foot, with the needle to the right so that the foot holds the fabric and you can guide the stitching.

3 Stitch slowly to maintain an accurate distance from the edge.

TIP *Add a row of edge stitching close to the garment edge to keep the facings from rolling to the outside.*

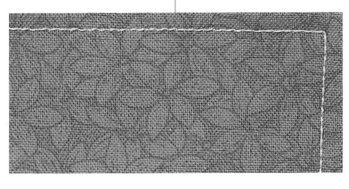

Top stitch

Used as a decorative surface finish, top stitching is an extra row of stitching. It can also be functional—to hold seam allowances flat, keep facings in place, to attach patch pockets, or for machine-stitched hems. ▼

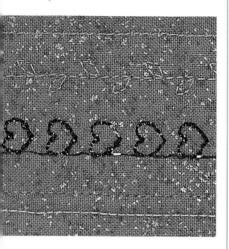

1 Use a contrasting colored thread if you want the stitching to be noticeable.

2 Stitch with a slightly longer than usual stitch length of 3–5 mm (about 5–9 stitches per in).

3 Use a stitching guide to keep stitching straight, for instance, the edge of the fabric. Alternatively place a piece of masking tape in the correct position on the footplate.

4 Decrease stitch length slightly when going round curves.

5 At corners, stop with the needle down, lift presser foot and pivot fabric. Put presser foot down and continue.

6 Stitch slowly and carefully to maintain accuracy.

Reinforced stitching

Used to strengthen areas where extra pressure may be applied or where the fabric is trimmed close to the stitching such as corners or curves.

Reduce the stitch length to 1.5mm (18–20 per in) and stitch 1 in (25mm) either side of the curve or corner, over the seam line. ▼

Machine basting

This is used to hold fabric layers together quickly but temporarily. These stitches will be removed once the seam is sewn permanently, so do not need to be fixed at either end.

1 Use a contrasting colored thread and select the longest straight stitch available.

2 Pin layers together, matching raw edges and then machine stitch along the seam line. ▼

Zigzag stitch

This can be used to neaten raw edges or to stitch a seam in a knit fabric that needs flexibility. ▼

1 Select zigzag stitch on your sewing machine.

2 Alter the width to reduce the stitch size from side to side.

3 Alter the length to set the distance between stitches.

Satin stitch

This is a very close zigzag stitch and is used to cover raw edges, apply appliqué, or for other decorative stitching (see above right).

1 The stitch length is set at a bare minimum (0.45mm).

2 Reduce stitch width to suit the application—the narrower the width, the smaller the stitches.

3 Test on a sample of fabric to check that the width and length chosen work together to produce tight, even stitching.

Stretch stitch

Another variation of zigzag stitch, stretch stitch has overlapping angled stitches and is used on fabrics that need stretch even after a seam is sewn. Many machines have a choice of stretch stitches to suit different fabrics. ▲

1 Select a stretch stitch from your machine's utility stitches.

2 Adjust stitch length and width to suit fabric—always test on a sample piece first.

Blind-hem stitch

This stitch can be formed by hand or machine. When stitched by machine it does leave very tiny ladder-like stitches on the right side of the fabric, but this will be almost invisible if the thread is a good enough match.

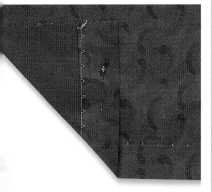

1 Neaten the raw edge of the hem allowance.

2 Fold the hem allowance to the wrong side and then fold it back on itself again so the raw edge sits to the right.

3 Select a blind hem foot. This has a larger left toe (with a metal fabric guide) and a shorter right toe.

4 Position the fabric under the presser foot, with fabric guide along the folded edge.

5 Select a blind hem stitch that will stitch mainly on the right single layer, and occasionally catch the folded fabric as it is guided through.

Shell stitch

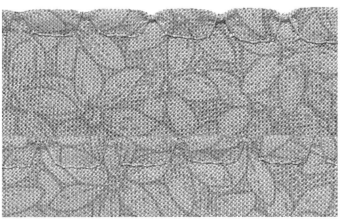

This is one of many decorative stitches used to finish a hem edge. It is similar to blind hemming but is worked at the fabric edge. It is most effective when stitched on bias-cut fabric or knits and soft, silky woven fabrics. ▲

1 If necessary, neaten raw edge of hem allowance.

2 Turn under hem allowance.

3 Select a satin-stitch foot, and place the folded edge of fabric along the slit of the foot so the right swing of the needle falls off the edge of the fabric.

Heirloom stitching

This is the term used to describe decorative stitching that has a traditional feel to it. Heirloom stitching is used on christening gowns and luxury tableware. It is usually made with a double or wing needle (which is designed to make holes as well as stitch). ▼

1 Use either a wing or a double-wing needle.

2 Select decorative stitches that work in and out of the same spot (such as pin, daisy, or star stitch).

French tacks

These are used to hold free-hanging linings to main garments and are stitched close to hem edges.

1 Take two or three long stitches between garment and lining (approximately 1 in [25mm] long). ▼

2 Blanket stitch over the two or three threads to hold them securely together.

Bar tacks

Two or three small straight stitches are taken on the spot. Bar tacks are used to stop zippers coming off the end or to finish ends of buttonholes.

COMMON SEWING TERMS

To help you with general sewing, fitting, and finishing, it is useful to know the most commonly used terms.

Grain

All woven fabrics have a grain—the direction of the weave. Straight grain or lengthwise grain is the term given to the threads running parallel with the selvages (side edges). This is the most stable, least stretchy grain and is used for most garment pieces.

The crosswise grain runs across from selvage to selvage, at right angles to the lengthwise grain. Fabric will stretch more on this grainline than on the lengthwise one.

The bias is any diagonal direction. Fabric stretches much more on the bias. True bias is found when the crosswise and lengthwise grain come together at a 45-degree angle. The true bias has the greatest stretch.

Nap

Nap is the term used to indicate that a fabric has a texture or design that goes one way and must therefore be cut and sewn in the same direction on all pieces of a finished project or garment. ▼

Fabrics "with nap" include those with pile such as fur fabrics, velvets, etc. Brushed one way they are smooth, the other and they are ruffled. More fabric is needed for a "with nap" layouts.

* Treat fabrics with a sheen or satin finish as if they have nap as they may reflect the light differently when held one way or the other.

* Patterned fabrics with a one-way design, checks, or plaids should also be treated as if they

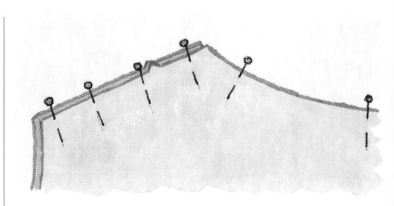

have a nap so that all the top parts of garments, drapes, etc. are the same.

* Cut each pattern piece from a single layer of fabric to ensure all pieces are cut in the right direction.

* Make sure the top end of each panel and the pattern piece are pointing in the same direction.

Without nap

As the name suggests this term is the opposite of "with nap." There will be no shading or textural difference when you run your hand over the fabric.

TIP *Use fabrics with the nap down for better wear.*

Pin basting

This is a quick method of keeping two or more layers together prior to stitching. It is an alternative to hand or machine basting, and is removed as the seams are stitched. Use pin basting for long straight seams. Thread basting is preferable on tricky areas such as matching neck edges to collars, sleeve heads to sleeves, etc.

1 Use pins with plastic or glass heads for easy removal. Paper clips are a good substitute for bulky fabrics or those that may mark, such as vinyl or leather.

2 Place pins at right angles to the seam so they are easily removed. On straight seams, place pins 5–6 in (13–15cm) apart. On slippery fabrics, increase pinning to every 2–3 in (5–8cm). ▲

Smooth nap

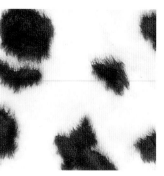

Ruffled nap

TIP *Some commercial patterns print directional arrows for stay stitching— follow these where applicable.*

3 Remove each pin as you come to it. Avoid stitching over the pin as it may damage or break the needle.

4 When cutting out large pattern pieces or drapes, use pattern weights or tin cans to hold fabric in place.

Cut on fold

Many pattern pieces can be cut on a fold so that two pieces are cut together, or one piece is cut and opened out for a totally symmetrical piece.

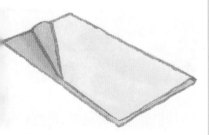

1 Fold the fabric evenly with the right sides of the fabric together. Most pattern layouts call for fabric to be folded lengthways, with selvages matching. ▲

2 Pin the pattern pieces in place, matching the grain lines and fold-line markings.

Single layer

Occasionally it is necessary to cut pieces from a single layer of fabric, particularly when working with one-way patterns, stripes, or checks.

1 Work with fabric right side up.

2 If two pieces are to be cut from one pattern section, turn the pattern piece face down for the second side to ensure there is a left and right piece.

TIP *When it is difficult to tell right from wrong side, mark each cut-out pattern piece on the wrong side to ensure they are all used correctly.*

Selvages

These are the side edges of the fabric. They may be slightly more tightly woven than the fabric. If a fabric appears to have no right or wrong side, use the side with the raised holes or marks in the selvage as the wrong side. ▼

Notches/balance marks

These are triangular symbols on the cutting edge of commercial patterns that are used to help match two pattern pieces. Frequently used for matching front to back, side seams, etc., they may have one, two, or even three notches. The corresponding pieces will have the same quantity. ▼

1 Cut them outward, standing proud of seam allowances.

2 Transfer all placement and balance marks to the wrong side of the fabric pieces immediately and remove pins to avoid unnecessary pin marking.

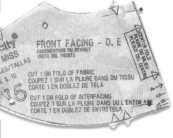

Directional stitching

It is preferable to stitch in the direction of the fabric grain in order to prevent undue stretching. The direction of the fabric grain can be determined by "stroking the cat." Run your finger along the cut edge and stitch in the direction in which the fibers curl smoothly.

1 Whenever possible, stitch in the direction of the fabric grain.

2 Always stitch all seams in the same direction—that is, from top to bottom or hem to top.

Stitch in the ditch

This is a row of stitching, worked from the right side, carefully stitched along the previous stitching by gently pulling the seam apart slightly as you stitch. It is used to secure facings, casings, and hem edges, and in quilting. ▲

1 Pin or hand baste facings in place, pinning from right side at right angles.

2 Select a slightly longer than normal stitch length (3–3.5mm, or 8–9 stitches per inch) and, with right side up, insert needle in the ditch created by previous seam.

3 Gently pull fabric apart to open up the ditch very slightly and continue stitching, removing pins as you go and catching facing in place on wrong side.

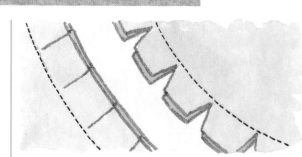

Clipping and notching

These are two terms used to describe how seam allowances on curved areas are cut to ensure they lay flat when they are turned through to the right side. ▲

Clipping On inner curves, clip into the seam allowance every 1–1½ in (25mm–3cm), cutting close to stitching. ▼

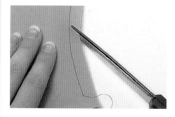

Notching On outer curves, wedge-shaped notches are cut out of the seam allowance. Again, cut close to but not through the stitching. ▼

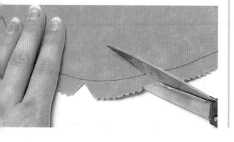

Grading seams

This is another method of finishing seam allowances and is used to reduce the bulk of the fabric in the turned seam.

1 Cut the seam allowance that lies close to the right side of the fabric to ¼ in (6mm).

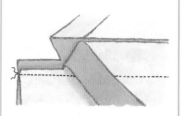

2 Cut the remaining seam allowance to a scant ⅛ in (3mm). ▲

Welt

This is the visible part of the binding on a buttonhole or pocket opening.

TIP Keep folded pattern piece with fabric piece for easy reference when sewing.

Pattern match

This describes the technique of matching patterns on right and left edges, often required for drapes, etc. and is used when working with patterned fabric, checks or plaids.

1 Cut each piece on a single layer of fabric.

2 Lay cut piece next to remaining fabric so that next section can be placed with pattern matching at key points (bust, hip, etc.).

3 Remember when cutting two of the same pattern piece, the second one should be placed face down on the fabric to ensure cutting a left and a right.

Pilling

Also known as bobbling, this is the term used to describe the tiny fabric balls that occur after repeated wear. They can be removed with a fabric shaver. The better the quality of fabric, the less it will pill.

Turn of the cloth

This refers to the amount of fabric that is taken up in the fold when fabric is folded into two or turned through to right side. It refers in particular to bulkier fabrics. The turn of the cloth must be taken into account when making self-fabric facings on jackets or for calculating hem allowances.

MAINLY DRESSMAKING

Godets Fabric inserts added to increase the swing and fullness of a skirt or dress.

TIP Use contrasting colored fabrics for the godet insets for a dramatic look.

Dolman sleeves Sleeves cut from the same piece as front or back, without a definite sleeve section. Also called kimono sleeves.

TIP Dolman sleeve designs are ideal for beginners as they are so easy—no sleeves to fit into armholes!

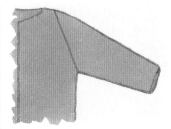

Raglan sleeves Sleeves that start mid-shoulder and are angled to mid-side, rather than set into an armhole.

Set-in sleeves Sleeves that are set into an armhole, with a seam on the shoulder end.

Plackets Fabric facing for openings in sleeve and neck edges. Part of the placket is folded to outside (see Collars and Cuffs.)

Gored A triangular shaped pattern piece used for a skirt that is fitted at the waist and then opens to a fuller hemline.

A-line Skirt that is angled outward from waist to hem, just like the letter A.

MAINLY SOFT FURNISHING

Headers The top of the curtain/drape. Header tape, also known as drapery tape is placed on the folded top edge, wrong side.

Swags Often combined with jabots, these are fabric sections hung across the window from side to side and then draped in folds or scallops. ▼

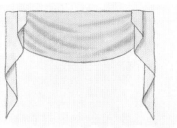

Jabots Softly pleated or gathered panels of fabric that hang down the sides of windows, usually with an assymmetrical hem. These can be full curtain length or finish half way. ▲

Valence A window treatment that can be used in conjunction with full curtains or on its own. It is simply a short curtain that covers just part of a window (average length is 10–16 in [25–40cm]). It is normally left drawn at all times.

Shades Usually with a straight top edge, shades are hung from the top of the window and are drawn up and down. Also known as blinds in Europe. ▼

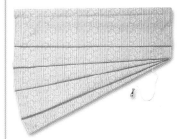

Pelmet A hard plywood version of the valence, it is made to fit above the window frame from side to side. It can be used to hide slopes, to make a window appear longer than it is, or be shaped for added interest. Pelmets are often covered in the drape fabric for a coordinated look.

Bolsters These are types of pillows and are usually sausage shaped. ▼

Flange/sham The term used to describe a pillow cover that is larger than the inserted pillow and has a top stitched soft edge. ▲

Piping The term used to describe a raised cord applied as a decorative edging. Piping can be made from purchased cord on a tape or from plain cord wrapped in bias strips of fabric. It is applied to the right side of one section before the front and back are stitched together. ▼

chapter two

ESSENTIAL SEWING TECHNIQUES

Essential hand stitching
Essential machine stitching
Easy tailoring
All about seams
Interfacing and stabilizers
Techniques for soft furnishings

ESSENTIAL HAND STITCHING

With time being limited, most sewing projects are done by machine nowadays, but there are still some occasions when sewing by hand is essential. Below are a few of the basic stitches that will cover most hand-sewing contingencies.

The first task is to secure the thread. There are three easy methods to do this—stitch on the spot, a knot, or using looped double thread.

TIP *Draw a chalk line along the stitching line, or mark it with pins, to keep the stitching straight.*

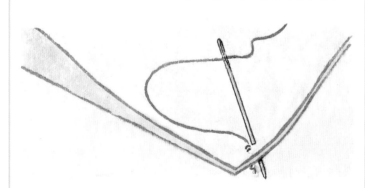

STITCH ON THE SPOT

This is quite simply 3–4 stitches taken on the same spot to secure the thread before and after sewing a seam. Start by taking the threaded needle through from the reverse of work to the front, until a tiny amount of thread is left at reverse. Then take the needle to reverse again, approximately ⅛ in (3mm) ahead of the first position and back up again to the front at first position. Repeat 3–4 times before continuing to stitch the seam. To finish, stitch on the spot again. End with thread at the reverse of work, pull up tightly and snip off thread ends.

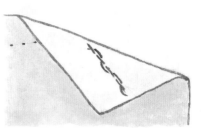

KNOTTED END ▲

Make a knot in the tail end of the thread, and working from the right side, approximately 1 in (25mm) from side edge, pull the threaded needle to reverse and back up again within ⅛ in (3mm) of the side edge. Start stitching using any of the methods below, catching the thread at the back as you stitch. Once the seam is finished, gently pull on the knot and snip off.

LOOPED THREAD

This method is only possible when working with a double length of thread. Use a larger-eyed needle and thread the doubled thread through the eye, pulling through until the loose tail ends are nearest the eye. Take the first stitch, close to the side edge, from the right

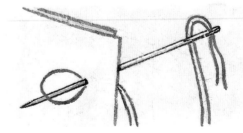

side of the work, through to the back and then up again to the right side, ⅛ in (3mm) to the left, and through the looped end before pulling up tight. ▼

RUNNING STITCH

This is a quick method of making straight stitches and is used to keep two or more layers of fabric together. It can be stitched with the stitches being formed in groups of three or more at a time. Note that there is a space between the stitches, and both the front and back of the work look the same. ▼

1 Thread a hand needle with approximately 22 in (60cm) of general-purpose thread and secure thread at one end of seam using back stitch on the spot or a knot in the thread end. At one side edge of the seam to be stitched, pass the needle from front of work through to the back and up again to the right side, approximately ⅛–¼ in (3–6mm) in front.

2 Repeat 3–4 times and then pull the needle completely through.

3 Complete the seam by finishing with back stitches on the spot. ▼

GATHERING STITCH

Gathering stitch is used to draw up a long length of fabric to fit a shorter straight section, or simply to gather onto a waistband, etc. It is a row of large running stitches. ▼

Use thread doubled for extra strength, secure it at one end with back stitches or a knot, and take 3–4 long running stitches at a time (each approximately ½ in [13mm] in length). Leave long thread tail at end. Pull up fabric to fit, adjusting folds and gathers evenly along the length, then back stitch to finish and hold gathers in place.

TIP *If a long length of fabric is to be gathered, split the length into 2–3 sections. This helps make gathering easier and prevents thread breaking under too much pressure.*

BACK STITCH

This hand stitch provides a finish that is similar to machine stitching, as once completed there are no gaps between the line of stitching at the back or front.

1 Secure the thread at one side edge (see above right) and then take needle through to back of work at the very beginning of the side edge, in one movement bringing it to the front, approximately ⅛ in (3mm) ahead. Pull up the thread.

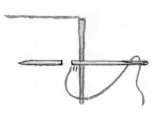

2 Take needle to reverse of work again at the same point of the first stitch (i.e. ⅛ in [3mm] behind) and up again to front ⅛ in (3mm) ahead. Continue to the end of the seam. Note on the reverse of the work the stitches will be slightly overlapped while on the front the stitches are close together. ▼

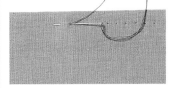

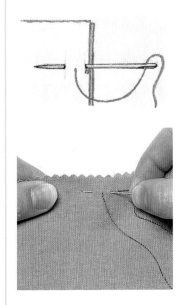

PRICK STITCH

This tiny hand stitch is virtually invisible from the front of the work and is often used on pile fabrics, such as velvet, when normal stitching can spoil the look of the pile.

On the right side of the work, the stitches are the size of a tiny pin-prick, hence the name, whilst at the back, they resemble running stitches. Prick stitch is a very similar decorative stitch used to add accent to garment edges. It is formed in the same way as prick stitch, working approximately ⅜–⅝ in (10–15mm) from the edge of the garment.

1 Secure thread at one end of seam to be stitched and then bring needle to front of work, taking it back to the reverse a very scant distance behind—literally 2–3 fabric fiber threads. ▼

2 Bring the needle back up to the front, approximately ⅛–¼ in (3–6mm) ahead, again taking it back to the reverse a scant distance behind. ▼

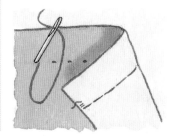

SLIP STITCH

This is another stitch that is virtually invisible and is used to secure hems to linings or to attach trims to main fabric.

1 Secure thread as usual. Pull needle through folded hem edge, then take up a scant 1–3 fabric fibers of lining or main fabric.

2 Bring the needle up through the folded hem fabric, slightly at an angle and in front of the last stitch. Repeat along the length that is to be stitched. ▲

WHIP STITCH

This stitch is used to secure two finished edges together, for instance badges to garments, ribbon trims to soft furnishings, etc.

1 Bring needle from the back of the work to the front at a right angle, approximately ⅛ in (3mm) from top edge.

2 Take needle back to main fabric, picking up 1–2 fiber threads before coming through to the front of the trim again. Work the stitches very close together. ▼

OVERCAST STITCH

Use this stitch to finish or secure raw edges and to prevent fabric raveling. It is similar to whip stitch, but the stitches are slightly larger and further apart.

1 Bring needle from back of work to front at right angles to the fabric edge, taking it back over the top edge to reverse, approximately ⅛ in (3mm) ahead of the needle position.

2 Repeat along the seam. ▼

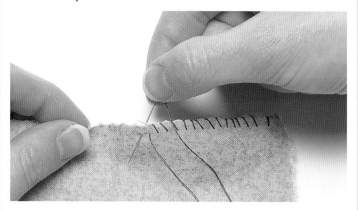

CROSS STITCH

This is used to hold pleats neatly in position on linings, etc. It is created by working two opposite rows of diagonal stitches. Note that while the front of the work shows the cross stitch, the reverse looks like a ladder.

TIP *Use a double thread for extra strength.*

1 Start from the fabric edge and bring needle through to the front of work at right angles, approximately ¼ in (6mm) from edge.

2 Take needle to back, diagonally, close to edge, approximately ¼ in (6mm) ahead of first stitch and then up to front again at right angles as before. Repeat to form first row of diagonal stitches.

3 Starting at the other end, take needle to back, again diagonally, but this time in the opposite direction to form the cross. Bring the needle up at right angles and repeat along the row. ◄

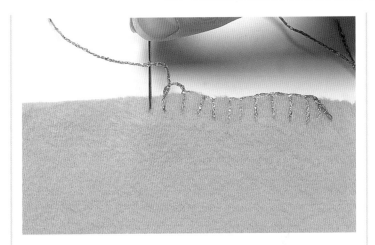

BLIND HEMMING

Similar to slip stitching, blind hemming should be virtually invisible from the right side of the fabric and is used, quite literally, to hem garments, curtains, and drapes. Hems that have been stitched with this technique are usually left unpressed at the actual hem edge to give a rounded, softer edge. Instead, just press gently, from the wrong side only, over the stitched area.

1 Turn raw hem edge under at least ½ in (13mm) and press. Turn hem allowance up and pin in position, with pins placed at right angles to hem edge.

2 Use a thread color to match fabric and, starting at a seam allowance, secure thread. Carefully fold the thread back, tucking under hem allowance slightly and bring needle through all thicknesses of the hem allowance. ▼

3 Pick up one or two fabric fiber threads of the main fabric before bringing the needle diagonally back through hem allowance, approximately ¼–½ in (6–13mm) in front. Continue stitching in this manner to the end. No stitches should show through on the right side.

TIP *After turning the raw edge to the wrong side, fuse a strip of edge tape to the wrong side of the main fabric within the hem allowance. Pick up fibers from the edge tape rather than main fabric when blind hemming to ensure no stitches appear on the right side.*

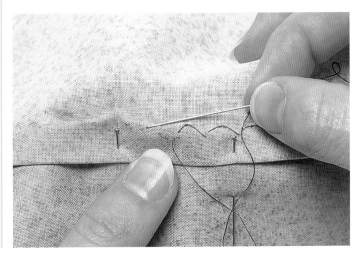

BLANKET STITCH

This stitch is usually formed at the edge of fabric and can be used to hold layers of fabric together. Starting from the back, left edge of the work, bring the needle to front, at right angles and approximately ¼ in (6mm) in from edge.

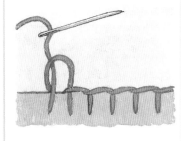

TIP *Use contrasting colored thread, embroidery floss, or thicker, buttonhole thread for a more decorative finish.*

1 Take needle to back, over top edge and bring it through to the front again, ¼ in (6mm) ahead, looping thread over needle.

2 Pull needle through fully so the looped thread tightens and sits along top edge. Repeat process along entire edge. ▲

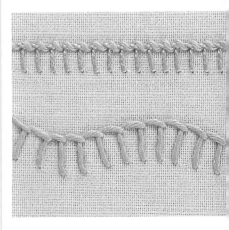

Although blanket stitch often has a functional purpose as a strong reinforcement, it can also be used decoratively on a variety of different fabrics. ▲

Basting

This is the term used to describe holding one or more layers of fabric together temporarily. There are two main ways of basting—pin basting and basting stitches, which can be done by hand or machine.

PIN BASTING

Pin layers together, matching raw edges and pinning every 2–5 in (5–13cm). Pin more frequently when working with slippery fabrics, or curved or gathered areas of fabric. Pin at right angles to the fabric edges so the pins can be removed easily as you stitch (see page 36 for more details). ▶

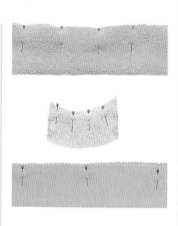

Basting stitches are large and are best done in a contrasting thread that is easy to see and thus easy to remove after the fabric layers have been permanently stitched together.

To hand baste, thread a hand needle with general-purpose or basting thread approximately 16 in (40cm) long. Tie a knot in one end, or take 2–3 back stitches loosely at one edge and then stitch layers together, with stitches ¼–½ in (6–13mm) in length. Work quickly by using a running stitch (3–4 stitches taken together). To machine baste, use the longest stitch length possible by adjusting the stitch length dial. Again, use a contrasting thread color that is easy to see and then remove later. ◀

TAILOR'S TACKS

These are the traditional marking stitches, made by hand stitching, used to transfer pattern placement markings from tissue pattern to fabric. Again, use contrasting-colored thread as they are removed once the markings have been successfully used to create darts, position pockets, etc. ▶

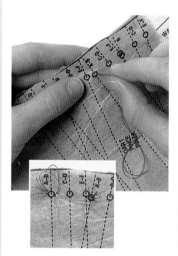

To make a tailor's tack
Thread a hand needle with general-purpose or basting thread and double the thread.

1 At the placement marking, with tissue paper uppermost, take the needle through the tissue and fabric layers to the back and up to the front again, leaving a loop of thread at the back and thread tail at the front. Repeat for a second time, again leaving a loop of thread at both front and back. Cut off thread, leaving another tail. Repeat for all pattern markings to be transferred. ◀

2 Separate the layers by cutting through the top loops and gently peeling away the tissue and top layer of fabric, snipping threads between fabric layers so that some threads remain in both pieces of fabric. ▶

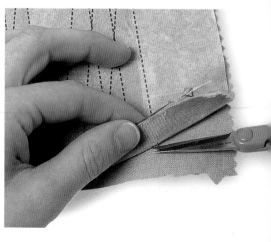

Adding beading and fringing

Adding decorative trims to garments or soft furnishings can give a new look to old fabrics, or jazz up plain ones, making them look professional and expensive!

BEADING

There is a variety of different beads and beaded trims to choose from nowadays. Individual beads or threaded beads need to be stitched on by hand, while beaded trims can sometimes be machine stitched in place.

Single beads

Use a beading needle, which has a very fine eye so that it will slip through tiny beads easily. It may also be curved.

• Secure the thread in a seam allowance or at the back of the work, bring needle to front, and slip on a bead.

• Pull bead close to fabric and then insert needle front to back almost in the same place it came from, bringing it back to front in position for the next bead. If beads are to be placed a little distance apart, make running stitches in the reverse of the work, catching just 1–2 fibers each time, so stitching will not show through. ▲

Threaded beads

These need securing at least every 2–3 beads, if not between each one.

• Starting at one end, bring needle up from the back of work between first two beads.

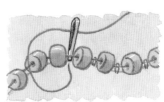

• Take needle to back, looping it over the thread holding the beads together, so that needle goes through fabric almost at same position. Repeat with needle between next two beads until row is firmly attached. ▲

Beaded trim

If possible, add beaded trim before finishing seams so that the ends can be captured within the seam allowance.

• Remove any beads from seam allowance by carefully cutting away, or crushing them.

• Match general-purpose thread color with trim, and use a small running stitch to hold trim in position but leaving beading to hang freely. If the trim tape is wider than ½ in (13mm), stitch along both long edges to secure in place. ▲

FRINGING

This type of trim is usually added to a hem edge but occasionally as a detail on pockets, shirt yokes, or pillow covers. Fringes with decorative tape or edges can be added to the top of a garment or a pillow cover, whereas those without finished edges are inserted within seam allowances, usually by machine during the actual project construction.

Surface fringing

Tuck raw edges under at either end of the trim to neaten, and place fringing in position (if at hem, place so that the fringing drops below fabric edge). Attach in the same manner as beaded trims.

For further tips and techniques on machine stitching trims, turn to Finishing touches, page 104.

ESSENTIAL MACHINE STITCHING

In order to sew soft furnishings and fashions successfully, a number of basic sewing techniques are required. So here is a step-by-step explanation for all the absolute essentials.

BUTTONHOLES

A necessary closure on many fashions and some cushion or chair covers, buttonholes can be easily made by anyone with today's modern sewing machines. Perfect buttonholes can be achieved whether you have a one-, three-, or more step buttonhole function on your machine, as long as the main ingredients are right. These include the correct mix of fabric, stabilizer, thread, and a sharp needle.

• **Fabric/thread** Any fabric can have buttonholes—from fine chiffons to stretchy knits. The key is to stabilize the area. This will prevent the fabric puckering or being pulled into the feed dogs. In most instances a general-purpose thread is adequate for buttonholes.

However, if they are to be a design feature, consider using buttonhole thread on coats, jackets, etc., and silk thread on silken garments.

• **Stabilizer** All buttonholes should have some sort of stabilizer included. This may be the interfacing between the facing and main fabric, a special waistbanding stiffener, or a layer of tear-away stabilizer. This helps when stitching, preventing puckering or pulling, and helps keep the area stable when buttoned up.

• **Needle** Make sure your needle is sharp, as buttonholes are made with lots of close zigzag stitches (satin stitch) worked closely together, so there is lots of penetration through several layers.

Making a buttonhole

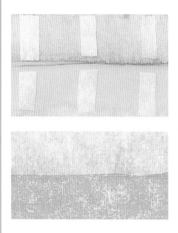

1 Interface or stabilize the buttonhole area by applying fusible interfacing to the wrong side of the fabric. Allow it to cool completely before continuing. ▲

2 If working without a pattern, determine the size of the buttonhole by measuring the circumference of the button (i.e. all around it). Halve this measurement, then add ⅛ in (3mm). Domed or novelty buttons require larger buttonholes to allow room for the shape—test on a sample first. ▲

3 Mark buttonhole positions at least ¾ in (2cm) from the fabric edge. If stitching a row of vertical buttonholes, use chalk pencil or thread to baste a center line from top to bottom of buttonhole area. Then mark each buttonhole length, at right angles to the center line, spacing each approximately 2½–3 in (6–8cm) apart (closer on very lightweight fabrics). On soft furnishings, the gap between buttonholes is usually 4–5 in (10–13cm). ▼ ▶

4 Set the sewing machine to buttonhole stitch. Most machines have one-, three- or five-step buttonhole stitches to sew one straight edge, bar tack at the end, back up the other edge, bar tack at the top, and then stitch on the spot for 2–3 stitches to fix the stitches. Check your user's manual to determine the type of buttonhole function you have.

5 Once satisfied, place the work under the presser foot and insert needle at the beginning of first row. Stitch out the buttonhole.

6 Feed thread tails into the close stitching before cutting off.

7 Open the buttonhole by inserting the seam ripper tool (quick unpick) between the two side edges and close to one end. Carefully push straight toward the other end. Insert a pin at furthest end to prevent the seam ripper accidentally going too far.

(If you don't have a seam ripper, use small sharp scissors but starting in the center, snip toward one end, again using a pin to prevent going too far. Repeat at other end.) ▼

For button loops and bound buttonholes, see Finishing touches, page 104.

> **TIP** When stitching buttonholes on fine, sheer fabrics, add an additional layer of tear-away or soluble stabilizer underneath the fabric. This will help prevent the fabric from bunching and puckering or even being pulled down into the feed dogs.

> **TIP** When sewing transparent fabrics, only interface the small area of each buttonhole, adding an extra layer of tear-away stabilizer under the fabric.

BUTTONS

There are two styles of button—sew-through and shank. The shank helps buttons sit properly when passed through layers of fabric. Sew-through buttons are used on finer fabrics, blouses, shirts, etc., but will still sit more comfortably if a small thread shank is created.

Positioning

1 Pin the layers of fabric to be fastened together as if the buttons are already applied and then mark button placement as follows:

2 For a vertical buttonhole, insert a pin ⅛ in (3mm) from the top of hole through to under layer. For a horizontal button, insert pin ⅛ in (3mm) from the outer end.

Sew-through

1 Thread hand needle with double thread and take a few back stitches at button position.

2 Holding a matchstick on top of the button, bring the needle up through the button and down again through another hole, sewing over the matchstick. Repeat several times. ▼

3 Take out the matchstick and pull button away from fabric, then wind thread around the excess thread below the button.

4 Return the needle to back of fabric and secure, before inserting the needle between fabric layers. Pull taut, and snip off.

> **TIP** Always test a buttonhole on a scrap of the same fabric with stabilizer in place to check it works properly. Some machines stitch the first row forward, others start stitching backward, which will therefore determine at which end of the buttonhole to place the needle to start.

Shank

1 As with sew-through buttons, thread needle with double strand of thread and take a few small back stitches at the pin position.

2 Sew through shank, catching fabric either side, several times. Again, back stitch on the spot to secure, tunnel thread between fabric layers, and snip off. ▲

For horizontal buttons, chalk or thread baste two parallel lines the width of the buttonhole apart, from top to bottom of the buttonhole area. Mark buttonhole positions evenly along the marked placement lines, 2–3 in (6–8cm) apart for garments, 4–5 in (10–13cm) apart for soft furnishings. ▲

If using commercial patterns, simply transfer the buttonhole markings from tissue to right side of fabric.

Zippers

Basic zipper insertions—such as regular, centered, or lapped zippers—are ideal for beginners. These are used in the side seams or back seams of skirts and dresses, and in soft furnishings, like pillows. These zippers do not show their teeth (or show them as little as possible), although the stitching holding them in place will be visible so a good color match is required.

The invisible zipper is a little more difficult to master but is perfect when you want a really neat appearance as the stitching does not show on the right side of the fabric.

Two types of zippers can be used for the basic methods— cotton or nylon zipper tapes and teeth. The nylon tapes are particularly suitable for bridal, childrens', and baby clothes. The cotton tapes are sturdier and suitable for heavier weight fabrics.

WHAT YOU NEED

• Purchase a zipper of the correct type (see right), length, and a good color match to your fabric. If the exact length is not available, cut to the length required and bar tack across the bottom to prevent the zipper tab coming off (see page 35 for bar tacks).

• For centered or side-seam zippers, the stitching shows on the right side, so a good thread color match is important. To test a color match, undo a small length of thread to hold against the fabric. If an exact match is not possible, choose a thread that is slightly darker than your fabric.

• Use the regular zipper foot supplied with your sewing machine and a medium-thickness needle (sizes 9–11).

ZIPPER TYPES

Conventional zipper

These zippers are open at the top and held together by a clasp at the bottom. They come in a variety of lengths and colors to suit any garment, and can be applied by the centered, lapped, exposed, or fly-front method. ▲

TIP *Ensure the top of the zipper is placed far enough down the seam to allow room for the facing, collar, or waistband to be sewn in place.*

TIP *Neaten the seam allowances, using overcast stitch or zigzag stitch, prior to inserting the zipper.*

Invisible zipper

This type of zipper is designed so that it disappears into the seam of a garment and is invisible when done up. It is perfect for skirts, dresses, and side-opening tops where the zipper is not designed to be a feature. As with other types of zippers, these can be purchased in a variety of colors so that you can ensure a good match with your fabric. ▼

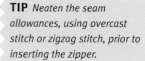

Open-end zipper

As this zipper is designed to open at both ends, it is perfect for jackets and zipper-front cardigans. It is usually sewn in using the centered method and you can purchase decorative tabs that add an extra design feature to the garment. ▲

TIP *Cut a larger than normal seam allowance—¼ in (2cm)—where the zipper will be placed.*

CENTERING A ZIPPER

This can be used in the back seams of dresses, skirts, and trousers, and in soft-furnishing garments such as pillow covers.

1 Mark the zipper length position with a pin or marker pen. (If using a commercial pattern, the position will be shown on the tissue. Transfer the markings to the wrong side of your fabric.) ▼

2 Baste the seam at the zipper opening down to the mark (see above right). Machine stitch the rest of the seam from the mark down to the hem then press the seam open.

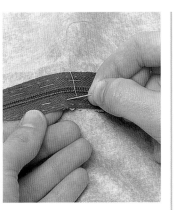

3 Place the zipper face down, on the wrong side of the pressed seam allowance, lining the teeth with the basted seam line. Baste the tape to the seam allowance only. Repeat on the other side.

4 Turn the work over. Pin all around the zipper through all thicknesses. Starting from the seam at the bottom of the zipper, machine across a few stitches through all thicknesses. Pivot with the needle in the work and continue stitching up to the top. Start again from the bottom and repeat on the second side. ▼ Remove the basting stitches.

LAPPED ZIPPER

This method is used in the side seams of dresses, pants, and skirts where the zipper is on the left side of the garment. This means that the lapped side covers the zipper teeth when viewed from the front. The lapped side can be put in by hand or machine. ▼

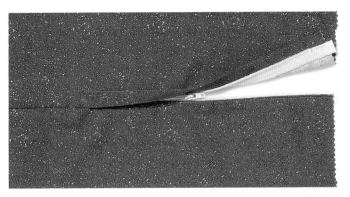

1 Mark the zipper position and baste the zipper seam together, machine stitching the rest of the seam down to the hem as before.

2 Open the zipper and with it face down, pin and stitch the zipper tape to the left seam allowance so teeth are along seam line. Pin and baste along center of zipper tape. Using a zipper foot, machine as close to the teeth as possible. Clip seam allowance below zipper end. ▶

3 Ensuring that the zipper is lying flat, pin and baste the right side of the zipper, through all thicknesses, across bottom up side ¼ in (6mm) from center of teeth.

TIP *Place a piece of tape along the stitching line as a guide line for your stitching. (You can use masking tape or quilter's tape.) Start at the bottom and work up to the top, removing pins as you stitch. This forms the lapped side. Remove the basting.*

4 Working from the right side, machine stitch or prick stitch by hand (see page 43 for prick stitching), starting at the bottom of the zipper.

CONCEALED (INVISIBLE) ZIPPER

A concealed zipper provides a very clean finish as it is stitched within the seam, so all that shows is the tab/slider. This type of zipper is usually lightweight and looks slightly different as the teeth are flatter and do not show from the right side when the zipper is closed. ▶

> **TIP** *A concealed zipper is inserted before the rest of the seam is stitched. This is the complete opposite to the insertion of a regular zipper.*

Zipper length—as with other zipper types, if the exact zip length is unobtainable, simply purchase one slightly longer than needed and trim as described above.

Zipper color—it doesn't matter if the exact color is unavailable because only the tab/slider will show. Choose a similar color tone.

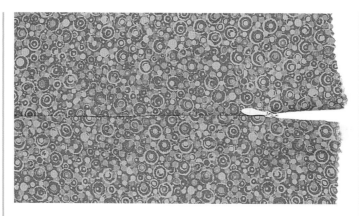

Concealed zipper foot—a concealed/invisible zipper foot has deep grooves on the underside so the teeth of the zipper slot into the grooves. Universal concealed zipper feet are available to fit most modern machines, but do check with your supplier as some machines will only work with their own manufacturer's feet.

Inserting concealed zippers

1 Allow extra seam allowance in the zipper area and, if applicable, at the top where the waistband will be sewn on to meet the top of the zipper.

2 Turn under and press both seam allowances of the zipper area, then open out again; this gives a straight line to work to. Alternatively, baste the opening together and press (basting will be removed later).

3 Place the open zipper face down on the seam allowance with teeth on the seam line. Pin and baste in place. (At this point, you can remove basting keeping seam allowance together if applicable.)

4 Attach the invisible zipper foot to your machine. Starting at the top, sew the first side of the zipper in place, stitching so that the teeth are in the groove of the foot and the stitching is as close to the teeth as possible. Stitch to within ¾ in (2cm) of lower end. Remove basting stitches and close zipper.

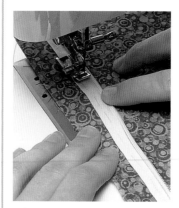

5 Repeat for the second side, pinning and basting remaining zipper tape to seam allowance as before. Open zipper.

6 Again starting at the top, sew in place, with the teeth under invisible zipper foot, stitching to within ¾ in (2cm) of lower end.

7 Pinning the zipper and tape to one side, baste the remaining seam in place from the stitching at foot of the zipper to the hem. Stitch, using the regular zipper foot. Make sure you do not catch the end of the zipper tape in the seam.

8 Finally, to prevent the seam stitching taking all the strain of the zipper being pulled, hand stitch the bottom of the zipper tape to the seam allowance.

> **TIP** *A regular zipper foot can be used but it is more difficult to obtain a neat result which depends on how close you can get the needle to the edge of the teeth. We do recommend using the specialist foot.*

Method with regular zipper foot

Basically you have to stitch as close as possible to the teeth of the zipper without catching them in the needle. Baste in place as before, position zipper foot, and adjust needle position, as close to the teeth as you can. Try to push the teeth to one side as you stitch. Continue in the same manner as above.

OPEN-ENDED/ SEPARATING ZIPPER

Separating or open-ended zippers are used on jackets, sportswear, etc. They are frequently made from heavier weight fabric and have chunkier teeth.

1 Measure seam allowances at top and bottom of zipper length to allow for facings/hems.

2 Separate the zipper and, using one side, pin it face down to the seam allowance on the right side of the fabric edge, so the teeth are along the seam line. ▲

3 Place facing, with right side underneath, over zipper and pin.

4 Using a regular zipper foot, machine in place. Start at hem edge, working close to the teeth. If applicable, continue up around the neck to center back. Repeat for the second side, ensuring the slider is moved out of the way of the machine needle. ▲

5 Clip seam allowances at corners and curves. Press and turn facing to the wrong side. Topstitch through all thicknesses if desired. ▼

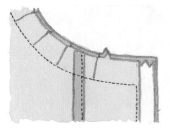

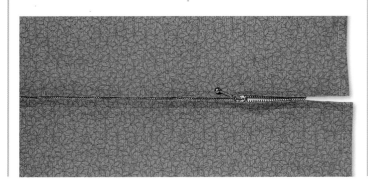

FLY-FRONT ZIPPER

These are often called mock fly zippers and can be right fly lapped over left side for women's clothing or left fly lapped over right for men. Strong metal zippers are a good choice for these fastenings (usually used on medium to heavyweight fabrics). Again a heavyweight needle is required.

The seam allowance or fly extension in the zipper area is usually wider than usual. Instructions below are for left fly lapped over right side, usually on men's clothing.

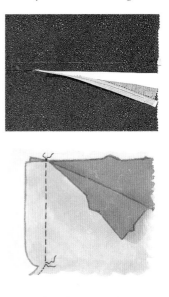

1 As before, baste the zipper seam to the bottom zipper mark and continue round crotch seam with regular size stitches. Clip seam allowance at the base of zipper. Interface the fly extension if desired. ▲

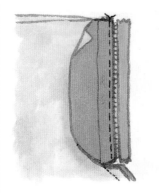

2 Fold right fly extension to the inside and press. Place the closed zipper, facing upward, under right extension, and with zipper teeth close to folded edge. Baste in place. (For women's clothing, fold left fly extension to inside.) ▲

3 Pin and baste the remaining zipper tape to left side extension (or right side for women's clothing). Stitch in center of tape, keeping the garment fronts free.

4 Spread garment flat and pin, with left extension to left, basting in place (for women's clothing, right extension to right).

5 Working from the right side of the garment, top stitch through all thicknesses. Make a guide with tape, pin and baste in place. Remove basting once stitched. ▼

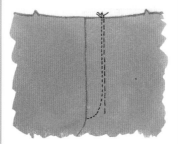

Applying elastic and casings

There are many types and widths of elastic, each used for different gathering techniques. Most common is straight-edged elastic, ranging in width from a mere ⅛ in (3mm) up to 3 in (8cm), used in gathered waistbands, as a partial fitting aid for pants, hats, around the neckline or waistline of gypsy-style tops, and to gather the top edges of bags, etc.

Elastic is inserted in a tunnel, called a casing, or applied at the same time as the casing is created, or simply machined to the inside edges. Generally, casings are used for outerwear, whereas for underwear, elastic can be added to the edges.

MAKING THE CASING

Casings are used on sleeves, pant leg ends, and to gather waistbands. Commercial patterns provide an extended garment edge with which to form the casing but, if working without a pattern, add approximately 2 in (5cm) to the top edge for the casing.

1 Press casing allowance to the wrong side, 2 in (5cm) from top, tucking raw edge under ¼ in (6mm). Pin or baste in place. ▼

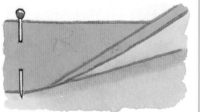

2 Stitch close to outer folded edge all around. Repeat for inner folded edge, leaving a 1½ in (4cm) gap in the lower edge to insert the elastic.

3 To determine the length of the elastic required, measure around appropriate part of body and deduct 1 in (25mm).

TIP *If using knit or stretch fabric, tucking raw edge under is unnecessary. For bulky fabrics, overcast or overlock the raw edge rather than tucking under to reduce bulk.*

4 Pin to anchor one end of the elastic close to gap, and using a large safety pin at the other end, feed the elastic through the casing, easing fabric along as you go. ▼

5 Lap ends of elastic by approximately 1 in (25mm) and then machine stitch together in a square.

6 Ease the stitched elastic ends into the casing and slip stitch the gap closed. ▼

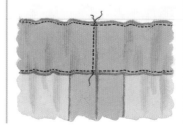

Applied casings

Applied casings are used at waistlines of dresses to gather the waist, or to minimize bulk on heavier fabrics or on shaped edges. These casings need to be flexible, so can be made from bias binding, tricot seam binding tapes, or even bias-cut lightweight fabric (on which edges will need neatening).

1 Cut bias tape the length required (to go around the ungathered garment), plus 1½ in (3cm).

2 Pin tape in position at waistline, top edge, etc., overlapping ends. If necessary, tuck raw edges of top layer under.

3 Stitch along both long edges, working both rows of stitching in the same direction. ▼

TIP *Before machine stitching, pin lapped ends together and try garment on for size. Adjust as necessary.*

TIP *If there are a few seams within casing position, prevent elastic getting stuck during insertion by applying a little fusible web to hold the seam allowances down within the casing area.*

4 Calculate the length of elastic required (as above) and insert where tape ends overlap.

ELASTIC APPLIED DIRECTLY

This method is used on the edges of knitted garments, shorts, sportswear, and lingerie. The elastic is stitched to the top edge of fabric, which is then folded down to form the casing (this also prevents the elastic curling or twisting). It uses the "quartering" method of application.

1 Determine the elastic length required (as above). Overlap the ends and machine stitch together to form a circle of elastic.

2 Neaten seam allowance of top edge of fabric and then divide it into quarters, marking with pins (i.e. side seams, center front, and back).

3 Divide the elastic into quarters. Pin the elastic to the wrong side of the garment, at the quarter marks, keeping one edge of the elastic even with the raw edge of the garment.

4 Apply the elastic to the garment edge, using zigzag or a stretch stitch and starting at one quarter mark. Stretch the elastic as you sew, so the next quarter marks meet, and so on.

5 Fold the elastic to the inside of the garment and pin in place at quarter marks again. Using zigzag or stretch stitch, stitch through all layers, close to the inner edge as before. ▲

TIP *To prevent unwanted added bulk, avoid lapping ends on a seam.*

EXPOSED ELASTIC

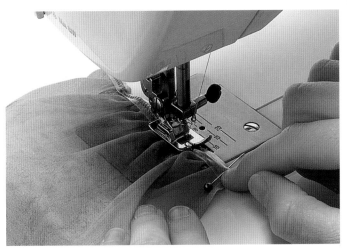

This method is generally used for lingerie, using soft stretchy elastic with a picot or decorative edge. It is easy to apply and comfortable to wear.

1 First neaten the garment edge by pressing the raw edge to inside a scant ⅛–¼ in (3–6mm), or using a small overcast or zigzag stitch.

2 Again, use the quarter method, dividing and marking the elastic and garment edge into quarters.

3 Place the elastic with the straight edge overlapping the neatened garment edge by ¼ in (6mm), pinning it to either the inside or the outside side of the garment.

4 Machine stitch elastic to fabric, stretching between quarters as detailed above. ▲

WORKING WITH A SERGER

Apply exposed elastic using a serger (overlocker), which will neaten the garment edge at the same time as stitching the elastic in place. With elastic side uppermost, pin in the straight edge along the garment foldline at the quarter marks. Place the straight elastic edge next to the blade and stitch carefully. Stretch the elastic as you work.

TIP *To help elastic sit comfortably and prevent it twisting within the casing, machine stitch at side seams, through all layers, from top to bottom of the waistband.*

Darts

Darts are used to add shape to garments at bust, waist, or shoulders. They help fabric mold to body contours and improve the fit.

Darts remove excess fabric in specific areas. They are usually single, wider at the outer edge, tapering to nothing within the garment, providing shaping at bust, shoulder, or waist. Double-ended darts are used at waistlines to add shape. They widen in the middle and taper to nothing at either end. Occasionally, the dart stitching line is curved for a closer fit.

MAKING DARTS

Dart placement and stitching lines are included on commercial patterns and need to be transferred to the wrong side of fabric sections using tailor's tacks or a marking pen.

Darts can easily be added without a pattern. The dart length on a skirt will be from waist to just above hip to provide shaping. On a top, darts are placed from side seam, just below armhole, to 1–1½ in (25–30mm) from bust point, and occasionally from waist up to mid-bust point.

SKIRTS

The difference between hip and waist measurement is the amount of fabric that needs to be darted out. Divide this difference between the number of darts to be used (usually two at front and two at back). For instance, if the waist is 30 in (76cm) and hips 38 in (96cm), the difference is 8 in (20cm), divided by four darts, equals 2 in (5cm) per dart.
If the excess (the difference between hip and waist measurement) is more than 8 in (20cm), increase the number of darts, i.e. four at front and four at back.

1 Mark the center of dart position, equal distances from center front and side. Use a pencil to mark the tip (in line with the hip) and then join the two outer points of dart at the fabric edge (equal distance from the center point of dart). ▲

TIP *Avoid having darts larger than 1½ in (3cm) at folded point in order to achieve a neat flat point at tapered end.*

2 With fabric right sides together, fold the dart, matching marked points at outer edge, tapering the fold to nothing at the tip. Pin in place, pinning at right angles so it is easy to remove pins as you stitch. ▲

3 Stitch, from the widest end to the tip, making the last few stitches right at the fold. To fasten off, stitch on the spot, or leave thread tails to knot. Do not back stitch as it may cause a ridge. ▲

4 Press to embed the stitches, avoiding pressing beyond the point, and pressing darts to the center.

TIP *When working with heavy fabrics such as woolens or fleece, cut open the dart along the fold, snipping close to the tapered end and press open. Dab a spot of fray check at the tapered end of fabrics that fray easily.* ▶

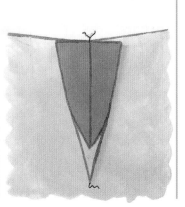

DRESSES

These may have double-ended darts either side of center front and back as well as side bust darts.

Bust darts are stitched as the skirt dart, with the widest end formed 2–3 in (5–8cm) below the armhole, tapering to nothing 1–1½ in (25–30mm) from bust point (sas shown at right). The size of the dart at widest point will depend on the difference between bust measurement at fullest point and chest measurement (just above bust, under arms). Stitch in the same manner as single darts, pressing fold down.

Double-ended darts are used on dresses to shape at waist line both front and back. The widest point of the dart is in the center.

1 Fold the dart in the usual way.

2 Starting at the center, stitch to one tapered end. Repeat from the center to other end. Again, fix stitches at ends or tie knots rather than backstitching to prevent ridges.

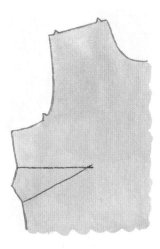

3 To help dart lay flat, clip folded fabric at center point and press toward center of garment. ▼

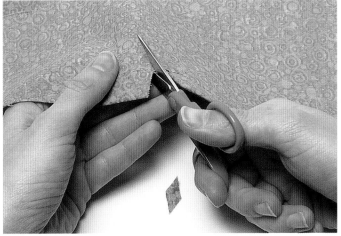

Pleats, tucks, and pin tucks

These add decorative detail and styling. They are formed by folding the fabric back on itself and thus a considerable amount of extra fabric is needed. The amount will depend on the number and depth of tucks or pleats.

Pleats and tucks have to be formed accurately—if you are as little as ⅛ in (3mm) out on each pleat, it could mean a difference of 1½ in (3cm) on a garment with 10 pleats.

PLEATS

There are three main types of pleat—knife/straight, box, or inverted. When pleating a skirt or dress, finish the hem edge first.

Box pleats are made up of two pleats, turned away from each other forming a panel. ▲

Knife pleats all face in the same direction, usually lapping right over left. ▲

Inverted pleats ◄ are formed with two straight pleats turned toward each other. They can be cut from one piece of fabric, or have the underlay section cut from a contrasting fabric.

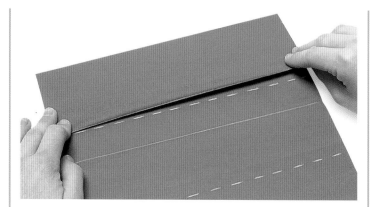

Making pleats

1 If using a commercial pattern, transfer the fold lines and placement lines onto the wrong side of the fabric. If working without a pattern, make a pleat template from stiff card, cutting it the width required for the finished pleat—i.e. 1 in (25mm) wide. Mark one edge as fold line and the other as placement line. Transfer these markings to the fabric area to be pleated.

2 If the pleats are to be soft and unpressed, mark these lines for about 2–4 in (5–10cm). For pleats that are pressed top to bottom, mark the lines along the total pleat length. ▲

3 Fold the pleat along the fold line and lap it to meet the placement line. Keep upper edges even to ensure pleats will hang straight and then pin in place at both fold and placement lines. ▲

TIP *Baste the pleats in place all along the fold line to keep them in place during garment construction.*

Caring for pleats

Always use a press cloth to avoid leaving imprints of the thick layers of fabric. Help pleats stay in place by stitching close to the inner folds of the pleat on the inside of the garment, particularly in the hem area.

For greater definition, stitch along the entire length of the fold on the right side of the garment.

TUCKS

These serve two purposes—as a decorative detail or as a useful fitting aid. Again, they have to be measured and sewn accurately to avoid taking in too much or too little fabric. The difference between tucks and pleats is that tucks are sewn in place along the folded edge.

Tucks are made along the straight grain of the fabric, parallel to the fabric threads. Vertical tucks are usually pressed away from the center front or back, horizontal tucks are pressed downward.

There are three main types of tuck—wide, pin, or corded.

Wide tuck—similar to pin tucks and pleats but wider. ▼

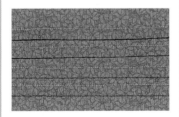

TIP *Use a different colored marking pencil or thread when trace basting fold and placement lines for ease of identification.*

Pin tuck—a very narrow tuck, often used on blouses, with best results achieved when using lightweight fabrics. ▼

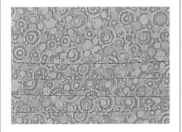

Corded—these have fine cord encased within the fold, which is then stitched in place. ▼

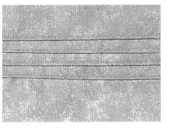

Making tucks

1 If tucks are to be folded and stitched to the inside of the garment, transfer markings to the wrong side of the fabric. If they are to be a decorative feature on the outside, transfer markings to the right side of the fabric.

2 As with pleats, if using commercial patterns, transfer the fold and stitching lines from tissue to fabric. Alternatively, make a cardboard template, cutting two angled notches for the tuck depth evenly spaced apart to indicate the gap between folds.

3 Place the template on the fabric and mark the tuck depth and distance between folds by lining up first and second tuck positions with first and second notches. Snip into seam allowance at either end to mark fold line and again to mark stitching line. ▲

4 Fold the fabric along the fold line lapping it to the stitching line. Press.

5 For tucks lapping on right side stitch close to the fold on the inside. For hidden tucks on inside, stitch close to fold on right side.

Pin tucks

1 Again, when using a commercial pattern, the position and fold line of the tucks will be marked on the tissue. If working without a pattern, make a narrow template the width of the tuck, i.e. ⅜ in (10mm).

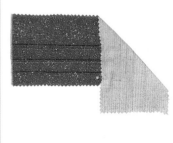

2 Transfer the fold line markings to the fabric by making a tiny snip within the seam allowance at either end or marking with tailor's chalk or a pulled thread along the line of marking. ▼

3 On the right side of the fabric, fold the tuck along the marked line and press in place.

4 For lapped tucks to be visible on right side, follow step 4 above.

Corded tucks

1 Follow steps 1–3 above, then encase cord within the fold on wrong side of garment and stitch from right side, close to cord using a cording or zipper foot. ▼

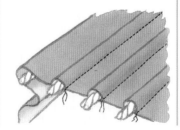

Easy fit with gathers

Fabric is gathered to fit a longer length onto a shorter edge, for instance on waistbands, yokes, to fit sleeves, or on hem edges of sports clothes, as well as to provide a fullness in drapes.

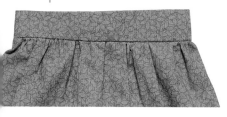

To gather successfully and evenly, follow these simple steps:

1 Use a contrasting colored thread in the bobbin so it is easily recognizable, and use the longest straight stitch length available on your machine.

2 Starting at one end, leaving long thread ends, stitch within seam allowance, to other end, again leaving a long thread end.

3 To gather, pull up the bobbin thread, (making sure the thread ends do not pull through), adjusting gathers as you go. ▼

4 Once the gathered piece and straight piece fit together, tie off the loose threads to keep the gathers in place, then machine stitch gathered section to straight edge, right sides together, matching raw edges.

CORD METHOD

This quick gathering method is ideal when working with heavyweight fabrics such as large drapes.

1 Cut a length of fine cord 5 in (12cm) longer than fabric length to be gathered.

2 Select largest zigzag stitch width and length.

3 Pin one end of cord, leaving a 2 in (5cm) tail, to seam allowance, pinning it ¼ in (6mm) from raw edge. Continue to pin it at intervals. ▼

4 Zigzag stitch over cord, being careful not to catch the cord in the stitching. ▼

TIP *When gathering long lengths—over ½ yd (50cm)— divide the gather stitching into two or more sections. Stop stitching after 18 in (46cm) or so, leave long thread tails, and start again to complete the row.*

5 To gather the fabric, pull up the cord, adjusting gathers evenly. Match gathered section to straight section as before and machine stitch, right sides together taking a ⅝ in (15mm) seam allowance.

6 Remove cord and keep for use again. ▼

TIP *Press gathered sections carefully to avoid crushing the fabric folds.*

Ruffles

Ruffles are formed from strips of gathered fabric and are used as decorative hem edges.

CUTTING THE RUFFLE

1 First, determine the ruffle size by measuring the straight hem edge onto which ruffle is to be attached and decide depth of ruffle. For lightweight fabrics and children's clothing, 1–3 in (25mm–8cm) ruffles are normal. Heavyweight fabrics, soft furnishings, etc. can have deeper ruffles, as much as 8 in (20cm).

2 Cut a panel 2–3 times the width of the hem edge by depth required, plus 1¼ in (3cm) for seam allowance and hem edge.

MAKING UP THE RUFFLE

1 Hem one long edge of the ruffle panel using one of the following methods: narrow double hemming (turn raw edge under ⅝ in [15mm] so it meets first fold; press and top stitch in place); machine-rolled hemming (using a rolled hem foot, machine stitch a rolled hem); lettuce-edged hemming (see Hem finishes, page 73).

2 Once hemmed, gather top edge by using a large straight stitch, stitched within seam allowance. Pull up bobbin thread, as described earlier, until gathered panel is same size as straight edge.

3 Turn up raw edge of main fabric at hemline, allowing ⅝ in (15mm) hem allowance. Press allowance to wrong side.

4 Working with right sides uppermost, pin hemmed ruffle to garment edge with the edge of the garment overlapping the ruffle, matching raw edges underneath. If necessary, adjust gathers of ruffle. Edge stitch close to the fold, stitching through all layers.

5 Neaten the raw edges of both garment hem allowance and ruffle top edge by overcasting, cutting with pinking shears, or binding with bias tape.

ADDING RUFFLES TO EXISTING HEMS

If adding a ruffled hem to a straight-edged hem, remember to adjust total length of garment so that it doesn't just become longer. Do this by marking the ruffle depth up from the garment raw hem edge. Trim off excess on garment, allowing a ⅝ in (15mm) seam allowance. Attach as described above.

ALTERNATIVE RUFFLING STYLE

An alternative ruffle style is to have a lapped top edge. To achieve this:

TIP *For gathers and ruffles, use extra strong thread in the bobbin (buttonhole thread) and stitch two parallel rows of gather stitches. Pull them up together, again using the bobbin thread.*

1 Follow step 1 above, then neaten the raw top edge of ruffle and hem edge of garment by overcasting or by using pinking scissors.

2 Fold neatened ruffle edge to wrong side, taking ⅝ in (15mm) seam allowance. Press.

3 Gather top edge as described above.

4 Working with right sides uppermost, pin ruffle on top of main fabric ⅝ in (15mm) from hem edge, so neatened edges match underneath. Top stitch in place, stitching ¼ in (6mm) from folded lapped edge. Remove gathering stitches and press.

Mitering

A miter, in sewing terms, is used to describe the neat treatment of angled corners on hem edges, patch pockets, or when adding trims.

There are two main methods of mitering—folded mitering, used on patch pockets, corners of table cloths, and hem slits, and trim mitering, used mainly when adding borders, braids, or ribbon trims.

FOLDED MITER

This method is also a neat and efficient method of reducing bulk at corners.

1 Cut the pocket to size required, allowing ⅝ in (15mm) seam allowance all around.

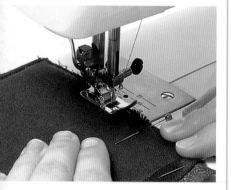

2 Stitch along the pocket seam lines and then press seam allowances along the stitching, folding toward the pocket. When sewing lightweight fabrics, leave out the seam-line stitching. ▲

3 At the corners, open out the seam allowances then fold up diagonally and press again. Trim this diagonal fold to ¼ in (6mm). Repeat on all four corners. ▲

4 Fold all seam allowances back to inside again so the folded edges at the corners just meet, forming a clean miter. Press. ▼

MITERING TRIMS

Every time a trim turns a corner, it needs to be mitered. There are two slightly different treatments for trims, depending on whether they are flat or fancy.

Flat trims

1 Pin the trim in place and top stitch along both long edges, ending stitching at the corner.

2 Fold the trim back upon itself and press. Holding fold in place, fold again, this time diagonally, so that it is at right angles and the edge is along the placement line. Press. ▼

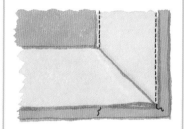

3 Undo the second fold so the trim is just folded back on itself and stitch along the diagonal fold through all trim layers. ▼

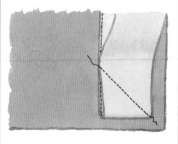

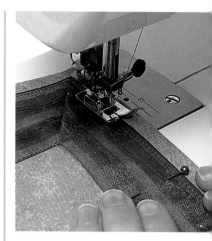

4 Again turn trim back down the diagonal stitching and press before continuing to top stitch along both long edges. Repeat for each corner. ▲

TIP *When sewing lightweight, crisp fabrics, for quicker results leave out the stitching along the seam lines.*

Fancy trims

These can be treated the same as flat trims, although the diagonal fold may need a little fiddling. Alternatively, fold as before, then carefully cut along the diagonal line. Fold the trim along the next long edge, matching the cut angled edges at the corner. Slip stitch them together.

Perfect pockets

There are four main types of pocket—patch, in-seam, side slant, and welt.

  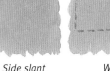 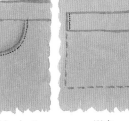

| Patch | In-seam | Side slant | Welt |

Patch—the shaped or square pockets placed on top of the garment at front or back (or side in cargo pants) and used on simple designs.

In-seam—a shaped pocket, placed with the opening in the side seams, used mainly in trousers and skirts, and some coats.

Side slant—positioned at hip level, part of the pocket also forms part of the garment (as in jeans).

Welt—a pocket that hangs on the inside with a lip or flap that is stitched in place on the outside (suitable for smart jackets, waistcoats and coats). Variations of the welt include jets (that have two thin lips) and flaps (that have one lip and a flap hanging down).

PATCH POCKETS

Probably the easiest to construct, patch pockets can be shaped, angled, or square, made in contrast or self fabric, and be lined or left unlined.

Lined pockets ▼

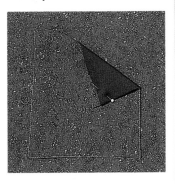

1 Mark the position of the pocket placement on the garment section, remembering to allow for seam allowances, facings, waistbands, etc. (If using commercial patterns, simply transfer the placement lines to fabric using a chalk pencil or fadeaway marking pen.)

2 Cut a pocket section to size, adding ⅝ in (13mm) on three sides and 1¼ in (3cm) on the top edge. Mark a fold line 1¼ in (3cm) from the top edge. Cut a lining piece the same size, and then trim 1 in (25mm) from the top edge of lining.

3 With right sides together, pin the lining to pocket section, matching sides and bottom edge. Turn raw edge of the top of lining down ¼ in (6mm) and press. Turn top edge of pocket (facing) down also, so that the raw edge meets the lining raw edge. Starting at the top right folded edge, machine stitch down the sides and across the bottom, taking a ¼ in (6mm) seam allowance. ▲

TIP Pockets can add bulk to the silhouette, so avoid side pockets at hip level if you have a pear-shaped figure.

4 Trim the seam allowance of the sides and lower edge. For square pockets, trim corners at an angle close to stitching. For shaped pockets, cut notches from the curved areas. ▼

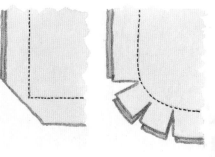

5 Turn pocket through at the opening in top. Press. Slip stitch the opening. Top or edge stitch the upper edge (if desired).

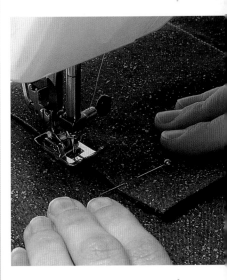

6 Pin pocket to the garment at placement marks. Edge stitch in place, stitching close to pocket edge, reinforcing at upper edges by back stitching a little. ▲

Self-faced patch pockets

1 Cut a pocket to size required, adding ⅝ in (15mm) on three side edges and 1¼ in (3cm) on top edge for the seam allowances. Mark a fold line 1¼ in (3cm) from top edge. Fold top edge to wrong side, ¼ in (6mm) from top. Machine stitch in place and press.

2 Turn neatened edge to wrong side along the fold line. Stitch at either end of flap. Trim seams within flap area. ▼

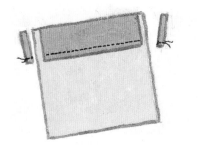

3 Turn in the remaining seam allowance at the sides, stitching as you go. For square corners at the bottom, miter (see Mitering, page 62); for rounded corners, ease stitch at curves, pull up thread and cut notches in the curved area to ease in fullness. Press.

4 Finish upper edge of the pocket with top or edge stitching. Then pin pocket to the garment and edge stitch in place, reinforcing the upper edges.

Self-lined patch pockets

1 Cut the pocket shape twice the length of the pocket plus seam allowances of ⅝ in (15mm) on all sides.

2 Fold pocket piece, right sides together, and stitch around sides and bottom, leaving a turning gap in the bottom. Trim seam allowances, cutting at angle on square corners and taking notches on curved pockets.

3 Turn pocket through to right side and press. Slip stitch opening. Finish the pocket and attach to garment, following instructions for the self-faced patch pocket.

IN-SEAM

These pockets are stitched at the same time as the seam is sewn. They usually loosely follow a hand shape, and are frequently made of lining fabric to avoid excessive bulk at the side seams.

1 Cut pocket to pattern, or draw pocket shape, with straight edges where it will join the seam. ▼

2 Pin straight edge of one pocket section at hip level of the side seam (3 in [8cm] below waist), right sides together. Machine stitch and neaten raw edge.

3 Pin side seam of skirt or pants, right sides together, pinning around pocket shape as you go.

4 Machine stitch from top to bottom and neaten raw edges. Clip into seam allowance of back of pocket/ garment; press pocket toward front of garment. Turn to right sides and press again.

SIDE-SLANT POCKETS

Also called hipline pockets, the slanted opening may be straight or curved. There are two parts to this type of pocket—the pocket (also part of the garment) and the facing. These pockets are not designed for the whole hand and thus are quite shallow.

1 Cut pocket facing from same or lightweight fabric. Cut front garment side edges at matching slant and stay stitch the opening edge or fuse edge tape in place to prevent unwanted stretch. ▼

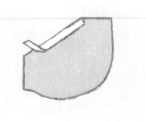

2 Stitch pocket facings to slanted side edges of garment front. Press seam allowances toward pocket, trimming seams. Turn pocket facings to inside along seam line. Press again, then edge stitch the pocket opening edge. ▼

3 From pant/skirt fabric, cut pocket section which will form part of the side seam and top edge of the garment.

4 Pin and stitch, with right sides together, pocket section to pocket facing, around the outer edges, keeping the garment free. Pin or baste at waist and side edges. ▲

5 Finish pant side seams in usual way, stitch from top to bottom, then add waistband and hems.

WELTS

Welt pockets can add a designer touch to plain garments and can be made in matching or contrasting fabric. Beginners should avoid welts on fabrics that fray easily.

Making welts

1 Firstly, the area to hold the welt must be interfaced. This is to stop the fabric from stretching and fraying when slashed and to make the cloth more substantial to take the weight of the pocket.

2 Also interface the square fabric piece that is going to make the welt. Choose either sew-in or fusible interfacing to suit the fabric weight.

3 Mark the welt position on the garment section and the top and bottom stitching lines for the pocket opening. (If you are using a commercial pattern there will be placement lines on the pattern tissue to transfer to fabric.) Then fold the welt section along the fold line and stitch down either short end. Trim seams and turn through. Press. ▼

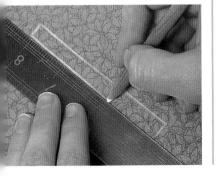

4 Baste the remaining long edges together, then pin and baste welt to garment along placement lines (matching seam line on welt with lower stitching line on garment). Machine in place, then trim back the seam allowance of the welt flap to ⅛ in (3mm). Press. ▼

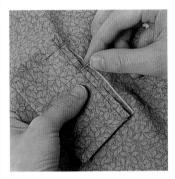

5 Cut a pocket section double the length of desired pocket and the width of the welt section. Transfer stitching lines to the center to match those on the garment. ▼

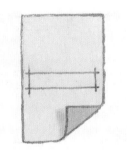

6 With right sides together, position the pocket section over the garment, matching stitching lines on the pocket piece and garment (note you are encasing the welt). Pin in place with half of pocket section above the marked lines.

7 Machine through all layers, starting at the center of the top stitching line (not on top of the welt) and stitch to just before the corner. The top row of stitching should be just one or two stitches shorter than the bottom row. Leave needle down in the work and pivot a little so that you will stitch at a slight angle to the very edge of the welt. Count the stitches down.

8 Stitch along the stitching line that holds the welt in place. Stop to turn at the very end of the welt so that the machine needle is on the outside edge of the welt. Count the stitches back up to the top row to ensure the same number as before, turn and stitch back to the center point.

9 Cut through the center of the rows of stitching, through the pocket and the garment. Snip right into the corners and then press before turning through. ▲

10 Push the upper part of the pocket section through the hole and press again. Repeat for the lower pocket section. The welt will come into place when you pull the two sides of the pocket section together. Press again. ▼

11 Machine stitch the pocket sections together, carefully keeping the garment section out of the way. To finish, hand stitch short ends of the welt in position. ▼

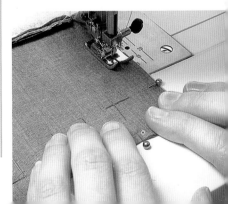

Waistbands

There are several different types and methods of applying waistbands. They may have side, back, or front openings, and be narrow or wide. The choice depends on the garment and look desired.

COMFORTABLE FIT

To fit comfortably, waistbands should be approximately ½–1 in (13–25mm) larger than actual waist size which allows for wearing ease. One end will also overlap the other (this lapped section has the buttonhole). Allow roughly 1¼ in (3cm) for the overlap.

CUT TO SIZE

Commercial patterns will have waistband pattern pieces for each size in pattern. However, if making a garment without a pattern, determine the waistband size by following these simple steps:

Length

For the total length, measure around waist and then to this measurement add:
* 1 in (25mm) ease
* 1¼ in (3cm) for ⅝ in (15mm) seam allowance at either end
* 1¼ in (3cm) for overlap.

Therefore, for a 26 in (66cm) waist, the total length of waistband will be 29½ in (75cm).

Width

To achieve the width of waistband required, double the finished width and add 1¼ in (3cm) seam allowances top and bottom (an average

finished width is 1½ in [4cm]). Thus, in our example, a finished 1½ in (4cm) waistband will be cut 4¼ in (11cm) wide.

INTERFACING

To help waistbands stay in shape and allow the garment to hang properly, waistbands need to be interfaced. How flexible they should be depends on the style of garment. ▼

There are many different types of waistbanding interfacings on the market, including those pre-cut to standard width, with perforations on seam lines and fold lines. These are ideal for cottons, polyester cottons, and wool mixes. For knits and stretch fabrics, a stretch sew-in interfacing is preferable. For a firm hold, try a waistbanding with attached stiffener, that prevents curling and creasing.

Apply chosen interfacing to the waistband. For fusibles, trim

the interfacing ⅝ in (15mm) all around so that it is not in the seam allowances. For sew-in varieties, baste just within seam allowance and then trim close to basting. ▲

REDUCING BULK

Waistbands have up to five layers of fabric—three layers of waistband fabric, main garment fabric, and lining. This can be bulky, particularly when using heavier weight fabrics. To reduce the bulk try one of these methods:

* Cut the waistband with one long edge on the fabric selvage —which doesn't then need neatening by turning under raw edge (remember to reduce waistband width by ¼ in [6mm] which would have been used in neatening raw edge).

* Neaten knit fabrics by cutting off ¼ in (6mm) while serging along one long edge.

* Interface just half the waistband with a waistband stiffener (such as petersham).

ATTACHING WAISTBANDS

Waistbands are added after zippers have been inserted.

1 Neaten one long edge of the waistband as above, or by turning under raw edge 1¼ in (6mm) and then machine stitching in place.

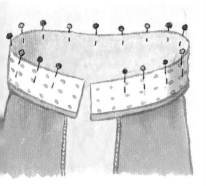

2 With right sides together attach the interfaced waistband to the garment, pinning ends of waistband to garment opening edges, leaving ⅝ in (15mm) overlap at one end and 1¼ in (3cm) at the other. Then find the center of unpinned waistband and center of garment waistline and pin together. Pin rest of waistband to garment edge, distributing fullness of garment edge evenly. (If working with commercial patterns, simply match notches and markings.) ▲

3 Machine stitch along pinned edges, taking ⅝ in (15mm) seam allowance. Trim seam allowances, grading them (see All about seams chapter) and press toward the waistband.

4 With right sides together, fold waistband at fold line, or so the neatened edge will just sit over the stitching, joining waistband to garment. ▼

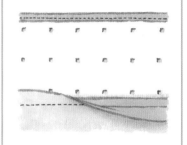

5 Stitch ends. Stitch from fold to raw edges taking ⅝ in (15mm) seam allowance. On overlapped end, stitch from fold to seamline, pivot with needle down, and then stitch along to where waistband is stitched to garment. ▼

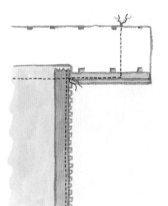

6 Trim seam allowances, cutting corners at angles. Also snip diagonally where overlap meets the garment. ▶

7 Turn waistband to right side along the fold line so the neatened edge overlaps waistband seam on the inside. Press. Working from right side, pin waistband layers together along the waistline seam.

8 Slip stitch neatened edge to garment at the seam line or, working from right side, stitch in the ditch or groove of the waistband seam, catching the finished edge of the waistband on the inside as you go. (As you stitch, pull waistband and garment apart so that stitching will fall within the gap of seamline.) ▲

TIP *If applying fusible waistbanding, use a hot iron and press cloth. Leave it to cool completely before handling again. This helps prevent the interfacing coming loose later.*

9 Finish by adding buttons and buttonholes, or hook-and-eye fasteners, as desired.

Facings and bands

Facings and bands are used to provide a neat finish at garment edges such as necklines, armholes, front and back openings. They can be made in the same fabric as the garment, or in a lightweight lining fabric for reduced bulk.

FACINGS

Most facings are created by attaching a separate piece of fabric to the relevant edge, but garments such as jackets may have a self facing—an extended front that folds back on itself to form the facing.

Facings are interfaced all over to add support and maintain shaping, while bands need interfacing applied to half the length only (as they are folded in half).

Steps to sew

1 Stay stitch the neck edge of the garment and facing to prevent unwanted stretch. (Front, back and armhole facings should not need stay stitching unless fabric being used is very stretchy.) ▼

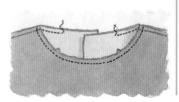

TIP *Grade seam allowances so that the one that will sit nearest to right side of fabric is larger than the underneath seam allowance. This reduces bulk, preventing an ugly ridge showing through the fabric.*

2 Cut the facings to size by following curvature of the neckline or armhole. The width will depend on the area being faced but an average finishing width is 2 in (5cm). Add ⅝ in (15mm) all around for seam allowance. ▼

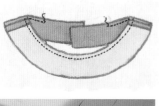

3 Apply interfacing, trimming it ⅝ in (15mm) smaller all around, so it is not within the seam allowance.

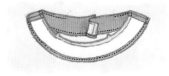

4 Neaten the outside edge by turning under raw edge and then topstitching or overcasting/serging the edge. ▲

5 With right sides together, attach facings to the main garment, matching raw edges. Machine stitch in place, and then trim seam allowances, clipping and notching at curved areas to reduce bulk and to help the facing lie flat when turned through.

6 Turn facing through. On most facings the seam will be on the foldline. For a neater finish, roll the seam line between fingers and thumb so that the stitching line falls just to the inside edge.

7 Under stitch the facing to the seam allowances to prevent it rolling to the outside. Press trimmed seam allowances toward opened-out facing, then edge stitch facing to seam allowances. Turn facing to inside and press.

BANDS

Bands are cut from straight strips of fabric that can be the same or contrasting color. As in the case of facings, the seam allowances are clipped and notched at curves to help the bands lie flat when they are folded over.

1 Cut the band length required plus hem allowance to match the garment hem. The width will depend on personal choice but, as a general rule, narrow bands (½–1 in [13–25mm]) suit smaller garments, jackets, etc., while wider bands, 2–3 in (5–8cm) suit longer/larger garments such as the edge to coats, kimonos, etc.

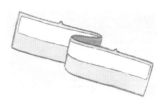

2 Cut and apply interfacing so it is half the width less ⅝ in (15mm) seam allowance.

3 Neaten one long edge and attach banding to garment.

4 Fold banding in half, right sides together, and sew ends together from fold to raw edge. At the hem edge, take the same hem allowance as the garment. Trim seam allowance and turn through. Press. Finish hem of garment in usual manner.

Collars

There are three types of collars—flat, rolled, and standing (or turtle [polo] neck). A flat collar lies against the neck edge. A rolled collar rises and then rolls down onto the garment. A standing collar is a band that rises straight up.

flat collar

standing collar

rolled collar

Collars have three layers, an upper collar, interfacing, and under collar. Sometimes there may be a facing also. On blouses and shirts, the upper and under collars are normally cut on the straight of grain, with both pieces being cut from the same pattern piece.

For a neat, crisp collar, attach interfacing to the upper collar section. As with interfacing facings and waistbands, cut off seam allowances on fusible interfacings, or trim sew-ins close to stitching.

Choose an interfacing that is lighter in weight than the fabric, as the adhesive may make it appear stiffer. Cut the interfacing on the straight grain (even if using a non-woven interfacing) as the incorrect grain will cause the collar to twist.

1 Trim under collar section so it is 1/16 in (1–2mm) smaller than the upper collar section.

2 Stitch collar sections together starting at the center and working to one end. Repeat for other side.

3 Ensure sharp corners on pointed collars by reducing stitch length just before and after corner, and taking one stitch diagonally across the point. Trim interfacing diagonally at corners within stitching line. ▼

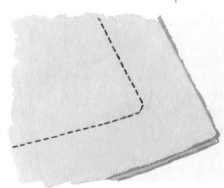

4 Trim and grade the seam allowances, notching and clipping at curved areas.

5 Trim the top collar seam allowance of medium and heavyweight fabrics to approximately 1/4 in (6mm) and the under collar allowance to 1/8 in (3mm), which will eliminate bulk.

6 Press stitched collar on both sides before turning through.

7 Turn through and ease corners out using a point turner.

8 Prepare the neck edge of the garment by stay stitching the curved areas. The neck edge will also require clipping and notching so it can be splayed out to accommodate the collar. The bigger the difference between the neck curve and collar curve, the more clips will be needed.

FLAT AND ROLLED COLLARS

1 Cut out the pattern pieces accurately and mark the relevant dots, notches, and roll lines on the fabric with chalk pencil or tailor's tacks.

2 On blouse, dress, and shirt collars, apply interfacing as previously described. For smart jackets, interface the under collar, with interfacing cut on bias. On rolled collars, add another layer of interfacing along the roll line on the under collar.

3 Pin and baste the collars together, and then machine stitch following steps 2–8 above. With the under collar side uppermost, press so that the seam is just showing on this edge (and doesn't show on the right side of the top collar). ▲

5 Under stitch as far as possible round a pointed collar—stitching the under collar and seam allowances together close to the edge, keeping the upper collar free. For a rounded shape collar under stitching is possible all the way round. ▶

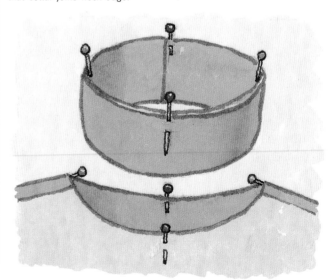

ATTACHING THE COLLAR

There are two ways to attach a flat or rolled collar—without a facing (usually used on blouses, shirts, and dresses), or with a facing (usually used on jackets or coats).

Without facing

1 Having stitched the collar sections together, neaten the remaining edge of the upper collar by tucking under ¼ in (6mm) and pressing.

2 Pin the under collar to the jacket, right sides together, matching raw edges and keeping the upper collar free. Machine stitch in place. Trim, grade, and clip seam allowances before pressing them toward the collar.

3 Fold neatened upper collar edge over seam and from the right side stitch in the ditch to secure, or slip stitch in place.

With facing

1 Pin completed collar to the jacket edge, with under collar side to the right side of the jacket and matching raw edges. Clip and notch the neck seam of garment to allow the collar to lay flat. Machine stitch in place.

2 Place the facing (on which outside edge is already neatened) right side down to upper collar, again matching raw edges. Machine stitch in place.

3 Trim and grade seam allowances of the collar and facing, then press them open.

4 Turn the facing to inside, encasing seam allowances and raw edges or collar. Under stitch the facing to seam allowances only.

> **TIP** *If the fabric is loosely woven or likely to fray, reduce the stitch length around the point to help stabilize the fabric in this area.*

STAND COLLARS

Stand collars are sewn onto the neckline, stand straight up, and are usually cut from a straight pattern piece. On woven fabrics, the neck edge of the garment will have to be well notched and clipped to accommodate the stand collar.

1 Interface stand collar section, excluding the seam allowances.

2 Turn one long edge under ¼ in (6mm) to neaten.

3 Pin and machine stitch the raw edge of collar to the garment neck edge, right sides together, leaving an overlap of 1 in (25mm) at one end.

4 Fold the collar, right sides together, and finish ends by stitching from the fold to raw edges, pivoting on the overlap section, and stitching to the point that collar joins neck edge.

5 Trim all seam allowances and press toward the collar.

6 Fold the collar the right way out and stitch the neatened edge to the inside garment neck edge, encasing the seam-allowance raw edges. (Or stitch in the ditch from the right side.)

STRETCH-KNIT COLLARS

On stretch-knit fabrics with no opening, stitch the short ends of collar band together to form a circle. Fold in half, wrong sides together, and then mark into equal quarters. Mark the neck edge of the garment in quarters and then pin, right sides together, raw edges of neck edge to collar, matching quarters. Position so that the seam of collar is at center back. ▼

Cuffs

Cuffs are like collars, separate elements of a garment, made from three layers—top, interfacing, and under layer, also known as the facing. Sometimes the upper and lower layers are cut as one and folded in two.

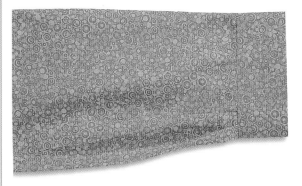

A cuff may have an opening, with a corresponding sleeve finish to match, or simply be a continuous band. They can be formed in much the same way as waistbands and stand collars. The types of sleeve finishes include faced plackets, continuous laps, and hemmed openings. The easiest is the hemmed opening.

Cuffs (or turn-ups) are also found on pants, shorts, or to finish short sleeves. The hem edge is extended and slightly shaped so that, once hemmed, the extension can be turned back up.

Rib-knit cuffs are a good way to finish sportswear on arms and legs, and are formed from tight, thick knit ribbing.

MAKING APPLIED CUFFS

This method creates a cuff from one piece of fabric, the fabric is folded to form both cuff and facing.

1 Use the pattern pieces provided, or otherwise cut a rectangle 6¼ in (16cm) wide by wrist circumference plus 2 in (5cm) for wearing ease and 1¼ in (3cm) seam allowances. Cut interfacing the same size less the seam allowances (see above right).

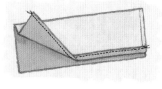

2 Apply interfacing and then neaten one long edge by turning raw edge to wrong side. If desired, top stitch in place.

3 Fold the cuff in two, with right sides together, so raw edge hangs below the neatened one by the seam allowance of ⅝ in (15mm). ▲

4 With neatened side uppermost, machine stitch side edges together, taking a ⅝ in (15mm) seam allowance. Press.

5 Trim seam allowances, cutting at angles on corners. Turn through, using a point turner to push out corners. Press again. The cuff is ready to attach to sleeve end, once the sleeve is prepared. The neatened side is the facing, and the raw-edged side the cuff.

HEMMED OPENING

This small opening is formed by turning up part of the seam allowance at the sleeve-hem edge.

1 Reinforce stitch the sleeve hem at the under arm side of sleeve, stitching along the seam line for approximately 2½ in (6cm).

2 Clip to the stitching ½ in (13mm) from either end of reinforced stitching.

3 Fold flap to wrong side, tucking the raw edge under to meet stitching line. Press.

4 Secure flap using fusible hemming tape or slip stitching. ▲

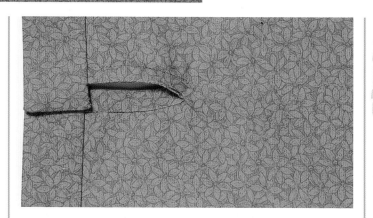

CONTINUOUS LAP

Cuffs on tailored shirts will often have an opening bound with a strip of fabric. This is applied before the underarm seam is sewn.

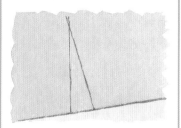

1 First create the sleeve opening by marking a "V" shape 3 in (8cm) long and 1½ in (3cm) wide at sleeve edge. The opening will be positioned on under-wrist side. ▲

2 Stay stitch along the "V" shape, stitching again over the actual "V" to reinforce.

3 Cut an opening between the stitching lines, snipping close but not through the point.

4 Cut a binding strip, 7 in (18cm) long x 1¼ in (3cm) wide. Neaten one long edge by turning under ¼ in (6mm).

5 Open out cut edges so that they are almost straight, and with right sides together, pin binding strip to sleeve opening, matching raw edges. Machine stitch in place ¼ in (6mm) from raw edges and then press seam allowances toward binding. ▼

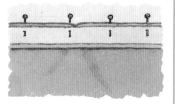

6 Fold binding to inside and slip stitch neatened edge over seam, encasing raw edges.

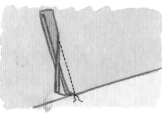

7 Press the front part of the lap to the inside and press in place (basting also if necessary). ▲

8 Stitch underarm seam together.

SEAM OPENING

1 Stitch underarm sleeve from top, stopping 3 in (8cm) from the sleeve end. Press the seam allowances open. ▼

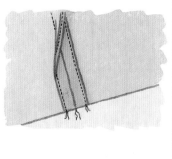

2 Neaten edges of seam allowances by turning the raw edges under and stitching in place. Press.

Attaching the cuff

1 Add the prepared cuff to the sleeve edge by pinning the raw edge of cuff to sleeve edge, right sides together, matching openings. Keep facing away from stitching.

2 Trim and grade the seam allowances and press toward cuff.

3 Fold facing to inside and slip stitch neatened edge in place over the seam allowances.

Turn to page 81 for sleeve plackets.

TIP *Do not trim and grade very lightweight or easily frayed fabrics as they may start to pull away from the stitching line when put under daily strain.*

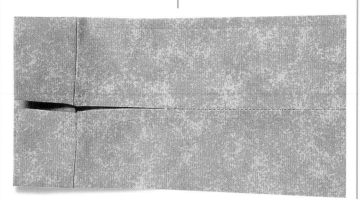

Hem finishes

Different hems suit different styles depending on the project, as well as the fabric being sewn. Here we cover double hems, top-stitched hems, bound hems, rolled and lettuce-edged hems, and blind hemming.

WHICH HEM?

Lightweight, transparent fabrics look stunning with a rolled hem, stretch knits take fluted lettuce hems beautifully, while cottons, wools, and drapes can be hemmed with double or top stitched hems. Suitings suit blind hems, while on coats or jackets (where the inside may show) try bound hem edges. Regardless of the hem finish, the basic preparations are the same.

Whatever method you choose, make sure that it works with the rest of the garment construction. For instance, do not add a top stitched hem to a garment without any other top stitching. Equally, a smart, pleated skirt would not suit a fluttering lettuce edge.

BASIC PREPARATIONS

1 If possible, hang the garment or drapes for 24 hours prior to hemming. This allows the fabric to settle, and even drop, and is particularly important for knit fabrics or those cut on the bias.

2 If sewing garments, try them on with appropriate underwear and shoes. These will affect the way the garment hangs.

3 Mark the desired hem level from floor upward. Place pins parallel to floor.

4 Turn up hem at marking, matching seam lines, openings, etc first. Pin in place at right angles to the hemline and then remove pins that are marking hemline. ▲

5 Measure and mark the desired hem allowance. The amount of hem allowance will depend on the type of garment—straight, medium-weight skirts/dresses can have up to 3 in (8cm) while A-line skirts and lightweight fabrics might have 1½–2 in (4–5cm). If necessary trim the hem allowance so it is even all the way round. Carefully press hem in place.

> **TIP** *To avoid ridges appearing on the right side, place a strip of brown paper between hem allowance and main fabric as you press.*

HANDLING CURVES

If the hem edge is curved, some easing in may be necessary. At curved edges, ease stitch ¼ in (6mm) from edge, using a slightly longer stitch. Gently pull up the bobbin thread. ▼

Alternatively, use a serger to ease the fullness. Use a slightly tightened needle tension and stitch, from the right side of fabric, 3–4 in (8–10cm) along the hem edge, bunching up the

fabric behind the foot by gently holding it there. Release the fabric and continue all around the raw edge. The hem allowance will automatically roll the garment.

FINISHING RAW EDGE

For fabrics that do not ravel, it is not always necessary to finish the raw edge. Cottons and lightweight fabrics can have the edges pinked with pinking shears. For other fabrics, the choices include: overcasting with one of the utility stitches or the zigzag stitch on your machine; serging the edge; or turning the raw edge under, and then pressing or binding the edge.

> **TIP** *When overcasting, test stitch lengths and widths on fabric scraps and adjust until the stitching lies flat.*

BOUND HEM EDGES

This provides a neat finish, ideal on coats and jackets where the inside may show. Cut the bias strips from self fabric, lining or otherwise use bias binding.

1 Cut bias strips 1½—2 in (4–5cm) wide and then join them together to form one strip long enough for the garment hem edge.

2 Machine stitch the bias strip to the hem edge, right sides together, matching the raw edges and taking a ¼ in (6mm) seam allowance.

3 Fold the bias strip over the stitching and press, then fold again to the wrong side, encasing raw hem edge. Press and pin in place, pinning at right angles. ▼

4 Working from the right side, machine stitch in the ditch—in the groove of the seam—catching the bias tape in place.

5 Turn up hem allowance and hand blind stitch in place, concealing the stitches behind the binding so they do not show.

TIP *Use the binding to finish off the side seams as well so all raw edges are matching inside the garment.*

HEM CHOICES

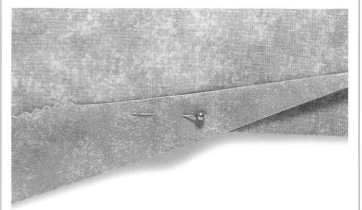

Double hemming

Suitable for lightweight fabrics, straight edges, drapes, table cloths, etc.

1 Follow the basic procedures to determine hem length—it is not necessary to neaten the raw edge.

2 Fold the hem allownace to the wrong side, folding again so that the raw edge meets the first fold line. Press. ▲

3 Finish by slip stitching or blind hemming.

Top stitched hem

Narrow top stitched hems are suitable for sheer, lightweight, and medium weight fabrics.

1 Fold the hem allowance as for double hemming. (Knit fabrics can have single fold only.) Working from the outside, top stitch close to the inner fold. Wide top stitched hems can be used on any type of fabric. However, avoid them on curved hems.

2 Fold hem allowance to wrong side (a good hem allowance depth is 1½–2 in [4–5cm]).

3 On woven fabrics, tuck the raw edge under ¼ in (6mm). Knit fabrics do not need this second tuck.

4 Working from the wrong side, machine stitch close to the inner fold or top of the hem allowance. Then machine stitch again, ¼ in (6mm) from the first row of stitching—working in the same direction for both rows. ▼

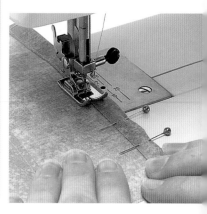

Rolled hem ▲

This hem is particularly attractive on sheer fabrics such as voiles, chiffons, and organdie. Some machines have a rolled hem foot with which to easily roll and stitch the fabric. However, when working with a normal foot follow these steps:

1 Mark the hemline ⅛ in (3mm) longer than hem length required then fold the hem up at this hemline—do not press.

2 Stitch as close to the fold as possible, then, using small scissors, carefully cut away hem allowance above the stitching.

3 Fold the hem again, along the stitching line, rolling the stitching just slightly to the inside.

4 Stitch again close to the inner fold.

Lettuce-edged hemming ▶

This is a very pretty, fluted hem ideal for lightweight fabrics and fabrics cut on the bias. It can be stitched on a sewing machine but will flute more easily if stitched by serger.

1 Follow basic preparations to gauge hem length, cutting hem to a scant ⅛ in (3mm) from hem edge.

2 Use a tight zigzag stitch and overcast hem edge, pulling fabric taut in front and behind the machine to stretch it as you stitch. Alternatively, serge edge with a slightly tightened needle tension, again stretching fabric as you stitch.

Blind hemming

Whether stitched by hand or machine, the aim of blind hemming is to prevent any stitching showing on the right side. This hem should also retain a soft rounded edge, so do not press the actual hem edge. To hand stitch, turn to Blind hemming, page 45. A machine stitched blind hem may show a tiny bit on the right side. To machine stitch, fold hem allowance up to wrong side and pin at right angles along hem edge.

1 Fold pinned hem back on itself so that ¼ in (6mm) of neatened hem allowance is on the right hand side. ▼

2 Use a blind hem foot and position so the needle just catches the fold of fabric as it stitches.

3 Open out the garment until the stitches lie flat and then press from the wrong side to set the stitches. ▼

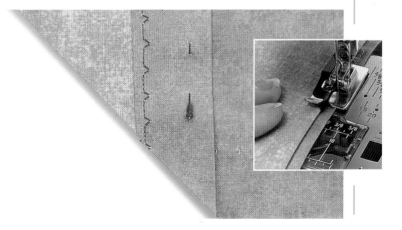

Smocking

This is a method of gathering fabric together in small, even pleats that can then be decorated with embroidery stitches.

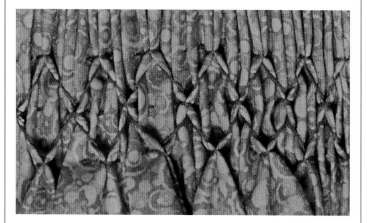

Smocking is traditionally done by hand, using embroidery floss/thread. Horizontal rows of long parallel stitching, worked from the wrong side, catching just a few threads each time on the right side, are pulled up to form tight pleats.

If a pattern calls for smocking, the pattern piece will be the required size. However, if you wish to insert a smocked panel into a cushion cover or dress, the panel needs to be at least three times the finish width required, plus seam allowances.

Suitable fabrics

Choose fabrics that are lightweight and that gather easily, such as cottons, batiste, handkerchief linens, crêpe de chine, Swiss cotton, or gingham.

Steps to prepare

1 Cut fabric the appropriate width (i.e. 3 times finished width plus seam allowances of ⅝ in [15mm] x the length required.

2 On the wrong side, mark with little dots, evenly spaced along the horizontal rows of the stitching lines (as shown above right).

3 Using embroidery floss, knotted at one end, start from the wrong side and insert needle through to the right side at first dot. ▼

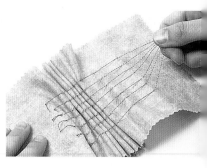

4 Bring needle back up to wrong side, just ¹⁄₁₆ in (1mm) in front. Insert needle again at next dot, making a long stitch between dots. Continue along the row. Leave long thread tail. Repeat for each row. ▼

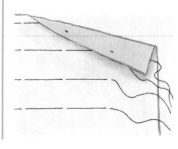

TIP *Make sure thread is long enough to stitch each row as it cannot be joined in the middle.*

5 Pull up all thread tails together, evenly spacing gathers and pleats. Pull threads until the panel is the correct width (plus seam allowances). Tie off or knot the thread ends. ▲

6 Working on a flat surface with the fabric right side up, smooth pleats until they are evenly spaced and then hover a steam iron above the pleats to steam press (do not let iron rest on fabric).

TIP Make sure the floss is held above the needle when moving down a row and below the needle when moving up a row.

EMBROIDERY DETAIL

Smocking can be finished with hand-embroidered surface stitches, worked from the right side. The running stitches creating the pleats are used as the stitching guidelines. There are a number of embroidery stitches that can be used for detail, including traditional diamonds, trellis, and van dyke stitch. Most embroidery stitches are made with three strands of embroidery floss.

TRADITIONAL DIAMONDS

Work over three rows of running stitches.

1 Starting at left side, bring needle up to front of work at outer edge of first pleat at first running stitch row.

2 Insert the needle again into the right side of the second pleat, and bring back up between the first and second pleats. Pull floss up to form tight stitch. ▼

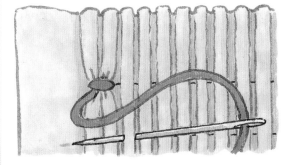

3 Drop down to the second running stitch row and take a stitch through third pleat, from right to left.

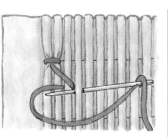

4 Hold thread below the needle and take the next stitch, still on second running stitch row, through pleat 4, from right to left. Again pull up. ▲

TIP Smocking stitches are often called by other names. Traditional diamonds, for example, can be called chevron or wave stitch. Trellis stitch can also be referred to as wave, chevron, or vandyke stitch.

5 Returning to the first running stitch row, take a stitch from pleat 5, right to left, keeping the floss below the needle.

6 Move floss to above needle and take stitch in pleat 6, again working right to left. Pull up floss. ▼

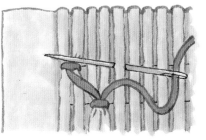

7 Continue across the pleats, working with the top two running stitch rows.

8 Make the diamond shape by starting at third running stitch row, first pleat, and continuing to stitch (as steps 1–6), working over second and third running stitch rows. Note that on the center row there will be two stitches formed at each pleat. ▼

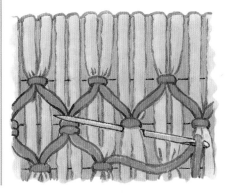

TRELLIS STITCH

1 As with diamonds, bring the floss up at left edge of first pleat, but at second running stitch row.

2 Take a stitch diagonally through the second pleat, so that needle comes up just above second row, keeping the floss below the needle.

3 Take next stitch in the third pleat, again working from right coming out slightly higher diagonally on the left. Repeat for pleat 4 and 5, so pleat five finishes at the first running stitch row.

4 Repeat in reverse over the next 6 rows, going down to second running stitch row. Continue all across the pleats.

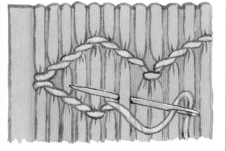

5 Again start at second running stitch row and work diagonally down to third row over five pleats and then back to second row over next five pleats. Continue across the pleats to finish. ▲

MACHINE SMOCKING/SHIRRING

A similar effect to hand smocking can be achieved by machine using shirring elastic either in the bobbin or couched with zigzag stitches.

1 Use two threads through one needle or use a thicker thread on the bobbin and work with right side facing down.

2 Stitch parallel rows of decorative stitching across the width as with hand stitching. ▲

3 Stitch further parallel zigzag rows between the decorative rows, couching the shirring elastic in place. Pull up elastic until the panel is the desired width. ▼

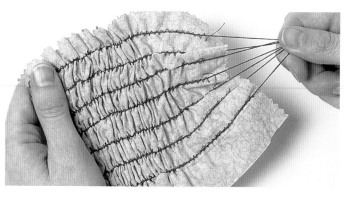

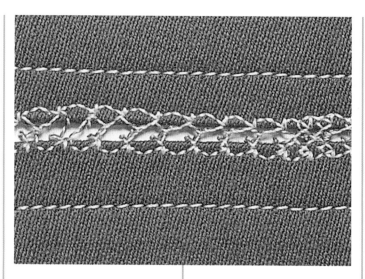

COUCHING

1 Use decorative thread in the bobbin and work with the wrong side uppermost.

2 Couch elastic down by using wide zigzag stitches, stitching over but not through the elastic.

3 Pull up elastic and adjust gathers on the right side before steam pressing.

FAGOTTING

This is another way of producing a decorative finish to fabric. It is a method of joining two pieces of fabric with a decorative stitch, leaving a space between the two fabric edges. ▲

1 Neaten the raw edges of the two fabric pieces to be joined and then turn the neatened edges to wrong side ½ in (13mm).

2 Select a decorative stitch on your sewing machine that incorporates sideways motion (zigzag action).

3 Pin a soluble stabilizer underneath the two fabric pieces, keeping them evenly spaced apart—no more than ⅛ in (3mm). Stitch, so the stitches catch the folded fabric edges on both sides by at least 1/16 in (1–2 mm).

4 Wash away the stabilizer.

EASY TAILORING

Tailoring is a subject all of its own, but there are still some simple techniques with which to add a tailored detail to jackets and suits. Here we cover how to turn a perfect reverse collar, add plackets or vents to sleeve hems, shape cloth, add linings, and bind edges.

TAILORING TOOLS

Firstly, a lot of tailoring techniques depend on perfect pressing, which in turn requires the correct tools. By using steam and pressing hams, you can shape fabric and press into awkward areas much more easily.

Tailor's ham

This is a small well-stuffed cushion with rounded ends over which curved seams can be steam pressed. They can be made from two 10 x 6 in (25 x 15cm) ovals cut from medium-weight cotton. Stuff very firmly to provide a firm surface on which to press.

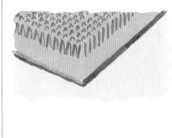

Pressing board

A shaped, usually wooden, pressing aid with iron-like appearance. It has a multicurved edge for pressing awkward shaped areas such as collars and cuffs.

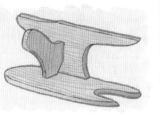

Clapper

This is a heavy wooden block used to pound creases into heavy fabrics after they are steamed.

Seam roll

This is a sausage-shaped, firmly stuffed roll of fabric, which is used to prevent small areas such as sleeves or trouser legs being pressed flat. Insert the roll into the sleeve and press seams over the roll. Again it can be made from two lengths of medium-weight cotton, approximately 17 x 3 in (43 x 8cm), stitched together and then firmly stuffed.

TIP *To improvize, use a tightly rolled-up towel wrapped in a pillow case.*

Needle board (or velvet board)

This is a pad covered with steel wires on which fabrics with pile can be pressed without crushing the pile.

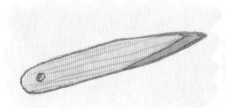

Sleeve board

This looks like a miniature ironing board and is used for pressing narrow areas that can not be threaded onto a conventional ironing board. The seam roll can be used for the same purpose.

Point turner

This ruler-shaped tool, with one angled end, is very useful for pushing collar points out and getting clean squared edges wherever necessary.

Pressing pad

This is a soft pad, made from two to three layers of wadding covered with fabric, on which to press embroideries or to prevent unwanted ridges when pressing.

TIP *A quick alternative is a fluffy towel. Use it folded for extra softness and place fabric pile side down.*

TIP *When interfacing forms just part of a fabric section, such as the back, cut the inner edges with pinking shears to prevent ridges appearing.*

INTERFACING

With the enormous range of interfacings available today, speed tailoring has become easier. By building up layers of interfacing at specific areas, extra stability can be applied as necessary, without the need to pad stitch layers of traditional horsehair, etc.

The new woven interfacings are particularly useful for tailoring. These are cut out in the same manner as fabrics—following the grain etc. (Turn to Interfacings and stabilizers, page 88 for more information on the variety of interfacings available.)

Reinforced areas

Add additional layers of fusible interfacing (matching the interfacing weight to the fabric weight) to lapels, upper back panels, under collars at the stand area, and at all hem edges.

Lapels

1 Cut an additional piece of interfacing to fit the lapel between the roll line and the outer edge, excluding the seam allowance.

2 Use a woven interfacing and cut with the grain line running parallel to the roll line.

3 Fuse to the interfaced front section, so it is a scant ⅛ in (6mm) from the roll line. ▼

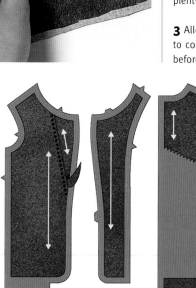

Pressing lapels

1 Place the interfaced jacket front, right side uppermost, on a flat surface.

2 Using the seam roll (or tightly rolled towel), roll lapel back over the roll and steam into shape by holding a steam iron a few inches away and applying plenty of steam. ▲

3 Allow the jacket to cool completely before moving.

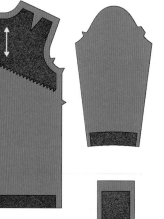

Under collar

Reinforce the stand of the under collar to add stability to the area.

1 Re-draw the under collar pattern piece, eliminating the center back seam by changing it to a "place on fold" line. Remember to deduct a seam allowance of ⅝ in (15mm).

2 Make a separate pattern piece for the stand section by tracing off the area between the roll line and neck edge. This is the stand.

3 Re-draw a grain line that is at right angles to the new fold line.

4 Cut out a new under collar section and interface all of it.

5 Using the traced section made earlier, reinforce the stand by fusing another layer of interfacing between roll and neck edge. ▲

Pressing under collar

1 Fold the under collar along the roll line and fasten to a tailor's ham so it is shaped as it would be around the neck.

2 Steam it into shape by holding a steam iron a few inches away and applying lots of steam.

3 Allow it to dry completely before removing.

HEM EDGES

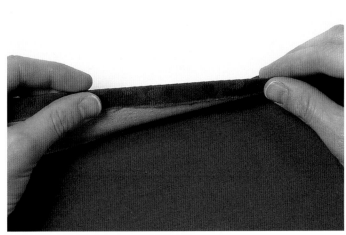

Add a strip of interfacing within the hem allowance and at sleeve ends to ensure a crisp, firm hem.

When using medium-weight fabrics it might also be necessary to add dress weights to the hem edges. These disc-like metal weights are added to the side and front edges of the hem allowance just prior to final hemming.

SPECIAL STITCHES

When finishing tailored garments, there are a few extra stitches that help achieve professional results.

Prick stitch

A version of back stitch, this hand stitch is used on fine or pile fabrics where stitching might spoil the texture.

Bring the needle up from the wrong side, then through to wrong side two or three threads behind first needle position before coming up about ¼ in (6mm) in front. ▼

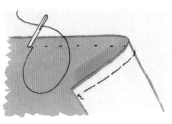

Stitch in the ditch

This is a method of holding two seams together, and is stitched from the right side, without the stitching showing. Align the seams together, or put facings and casings in place.

Then, working from the right side, straight stitch in the ditch by spreading the seam open with fingers. ▼

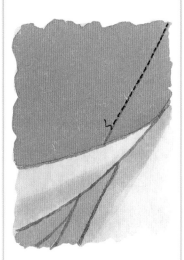

Under stitch

This is a row of straight stitching made to prevent facings from rolling out. The stitching is done as close to the edge as possible, through the facing and seam allowances only. ▼

SLEEVE FINISHES

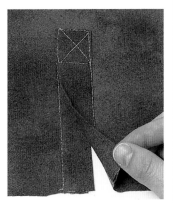

Plackets

This is a classic band used to finish sleeve openings or necklines of tailored dresses. It is created by adding a separate shaped and folded piece of fabric to the opening. Add sleeve plackets before stitching the underarm seam. ▲

1 Use the paper pattern pieces supplied and transfer all markings to garment opening and placket. Use a different color of marking pen or thread to mark the different types of dots for easier matching.

2 Position the placket on the sleeve (or neckline), with the extended section of the placket toward the front of the sleeve. Pin with right side of placket to wrong side of sleeve.

3 Machine stitch along the stitching line, working from lower edge up and across top, and down to other lower edge to make a three-sided box.

4 Cut up the center of the box, snipping right into the corners. Turn through to the right side of the garment.

5 Fold the shorter placket side, so it fills the opening, tucking raw edge under, and machine stitch in place. ▼

6 Working with the extended placket, press the fabric over the stitched side and back on itself, again tucking raw edges under. This side should lie on top of the stitched side.

7 Stitch carefully, avoiding catching the under layer. Again, starting at the lower edge, work to the top, pivot and across, and then down to where short side stitching starts (underneath).

8 Finish the upper section of the placket with a stitched "X."

9 Finish working the sleeve in the usual manner.

Vents

These are the overlapping slashes formed on jacket sleeves for men and women. Men's jackets will have buttonholes and buttons as closures while on women's jackets, the buttons are added as decorative detail only. ▲

A vent is formed on a two-piece sleeve—one with upper and under sleeve pattern pieces. It is constructed before the sleeve is sewn together. However, as it incorporates the sleeve hem, check the

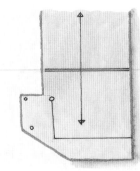

length of the finished sleeve before beginning. ▼

The sleeve pattern pieces will incorporate an extension on the lower outside edges. Transfer all the markings, stitching, and fold lines to the wrong side of the fabric.

1 Interface the hem allowance of the sleeve with bias strips of woven fusible interfacing that is slightly lighter in weight than the jacket fabric. Note that the interfacing should just overlap the hem fold line.

2 Fuse more bias strips of interfacing in the extensions.

3 Position the pattern tissue back on the fabric and transfer dots and fold lines again before joining the upper and under sleeve along the inner edge (non-extension side). Press the seam open.

4 One side of the extension will be slightly shaped—this makes the miter at top. Stitch the two angled edges together between dots, then trim to reduce bulk, and press open, as shown above right.

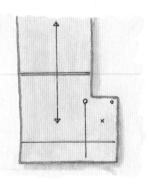

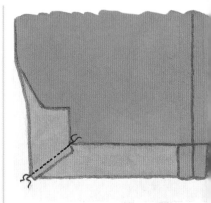

5 Fold the hem allowance up, right side to right side, and finish the opposite extension edge by stitching a small narrow seam ¼ in (6mm) wide along the depth of the hem allowance. Turn to the right side and press.

6 Complete the sleeve by bringing the remaining sleeve seams right sides together, and then stitch from just above the vent to the armhole. Ensure the sleeve hem is matching at the bottom edge.

7 To finish, carefully clip the seam allowance just above the vent and using a seam roll, press the sleeve seam open. Turn to the right side. The extensions should lie beautifully one on top of the other. Finish by adding with decorative buttons.

ALL ABOUT SEAMS

Seams are the mainstay of sewing—they hold layers of fabric together. Different fabric and different garments require different seaming techniques, depending on whether the under side will show through, or if the seam needs to be extra strong. We cover a range of seams and seam finishes to cater for every need.

PLAIN SEAMS

A plain, straight-stitched seam is the most commonly used seam for garments and soft furnishings. By varying the stitch length, different weights and thicknesses can be sewn with ease. For more about stitch lengths and tensions, turn to Sewing machines and sergers, page 18.

Getting started

1 One of the main problems at the start of a seam is the thread tails getting tangled, or the fabric being pulled down into the feed dogs. Prevent this by holding both needle and bobbin thread in one hand and pulling gently toward the back as you start stitching.

2 Hold until at least 1 in (25mm) has been stitched.

3 Continue to feed fabric evenly by resting one hand on front of fabric to guide it through, and the other at the back to keep it moving smoothly. ▼

Back stitch

Machine back stitches are used to fix the stitches at the start and end of a row. Most machines have a reverse button, which is depressed whilst reverse stitching.

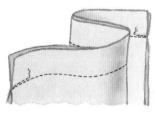

To back stitch correctly, insert the needle in the fabric ½ in (13mm) from the top end. Holding the reverse button, stitch backward. Release the button and continue forward, going over back stitches, until the end is reached. Again press the reverse button and back stitch for ⅜ in (10mm) over last few stitches. Feed the thread ends between the layers in the seam allowance, pull tight, and snip off.

Stitching guidelines

* Test the stitch length and tension on a combination of fabric layers and interfacing matching the fabric to be sewn.

* Stitch all seams in the same direction (i.e. from top to bottom) to prevent pulling out of shape (particularly important on stretchy fabrics).

* Stitch woven fabrics with a straight stitch, and stretch fabrics with a stretch stitch or zigzag stitch.

* Make sure that the seam allowances remain constant throughout a garment (see Seam allowances, page 84).

* To help with handling when sewing very lightweight fabrics or those with pile, use wider-than-normal seam allowances.

* Neaten all seam allowances to prevent unraveling.

* Cut corners at an angle, close to the stitching. Add a dab of fabric glue to cut edges if fabrics fray easily.

* Press each seam, first on the wrong side, and then from the right side to set stitches.

* Always press the seams before crossing with another line of stitching.

TIP *If fabric does still get pulled into feed dogs at the start of a seam, try a finer needle size, or add a layer of tear-away stabilizer underneath the fabric at the start of the seam.*

Maintaining accuracy

It is important to stitch seams evenly, maintaining the seam allowances that have been built in to each pattern piece in order to ensure an accurate fit. For instance, on a princess-seamed dress, which has two front, two back and two side seams (thus six seams in total), if each is inaccurately sewn by just ⅜ in (10mm) the total difference could be as much as 2½ in (6cm). ▼

Ensure seams are stitched accurately and evenly by using one of the following methods:

• Use the markings on the throat plate as a guideline of distance between needle position and fabric edge.

The throat plate is generally marked in ⅛ in (3mm) increments. If you require a different distance, position a length of tape the distance required from the needle as a guide.

• Use the difference between needle position and outer edge of presser foot as a guide. Most machines allow the needle to be moved to left, center, or right, which will increase or decrease the seam allowance.

• Working on the wrong side of the fabric, mark the seam line with chalk.

SEAM ALLOWANCES

This is the area of fabric between the stitching line and cut edge. Most commercial patterns include a ⅝ in (15mm) seam allowance on general dressmaking patterns and ¼ in (6mm) on craft patterns. The seam allowance allows room for handling, prevents seams pulling apart

with wear, and accommodates slight adjustments for fit. The seam allowances are neatened once seams are sewn—failure to neaten properly can result in seams splitting where fabric unravels, or excessive ridges at seam areas.

Reducing bulk

Seam allowances that are encased within facings, hem allowances, waistbands, collars and cuffs, etc., do not always need neatening but will need to be reduced to prevent unwanted bulk. To do this requires trimming, grading, clipping, and notching.

Trimming

Once the seam has been sewn and pressed, cut seam allowances to a minimal ¼ in (6mm). Trim corners at an angle, close to the stitching. ▲

Grading

This reducing technique is used on bulky fabrics, where the seam allowances may cause a visible ridge on the right side of the fabric. The two seam allowances are cut at different widths to decrease the bulk. The seam allowance that lies closest to the inside is trimmed to a scant ⅛ in (3mm) and the remaining seam allowance, which will lie closest to the outside of the garment, is trimmed to ¼ in (6mm). ▲

TIP *If fabric tends to ravel, dab a spot of fabric glue on corner stitching.*

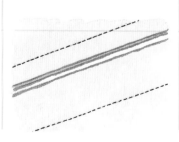

Clipping and notching

These terms describe the technique of reducing bulk at curves and allowing fabric to spread and lie flat. Sometimes it is necessary to clip seam allowances on curved areas before stitching two pieces together in order to fit the pieces accurately.

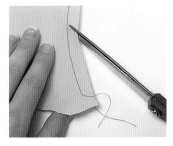

1 Stay stitch curved area of fabric, just within the seam allowance.

2 At inside curves (those that are concave) make little clips or snips in the seam allowance. ▲

3 On outward or convex curves, cut wedge-shaped notches from the seam allowance to allow the fabric to spread around the curve when turned through. This also eliminates excess fabric from the seam area. ▼

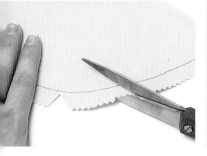

SEAM NEATENING

Seam allowances that are not encased need to be neatened to prevent raveling and provide a professional finish. There are a number of ways to neaten the seams, depending on the fabric type and thickness, and whether the wrong side will show. The quickest and easiest method is to pink the raw edges using pinking shears. Another quick method is to overlock on a serger, or overcast with zigzag stitching. A neat option, where the seam finishes will be visible, is to bind the edges.

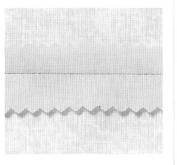

Pinked edges

Having stitched and pressed the seam, use pinking shears to trim seam allowances on both layers to within ¼ in (6mm) of seam. Press again with seam allowances pressed together on one side on lightweight fabrics, and pressed open on heavier weight fabrics. ▲

Overcasting/overstitching

Using an overcast stitch or zigzag stitch and working with the right edge of the seam allowance just caught by the needle, stitch over raw edges. Again, seam allowances on lightweight fabrics can be stitched together, but heavier weight fabrics need each layer stitched separately. Alternatively, use a serger to overlock and trim the edges in one pass.

Bound edges

This method is suitable for any fabric type and provides a very neat finish that doesn't look unsightly if visible from the right side. The edges can be bound with bias binding, or a special sheer lightweight seam binding tape. These specialist tapes will fold in two when gently pulled making them very easy to use. ▲

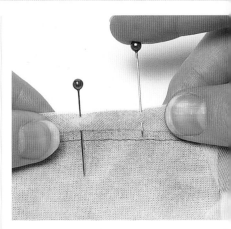

1 Slightly tug the stretch binding to see which way it curls, and then wrap around raw edges and pin at top to secure in place. ▲

2 Gently pull on the tape so it curls over the raw edges as you stitch. As you sew, you will stitch through both layers of tape at once.

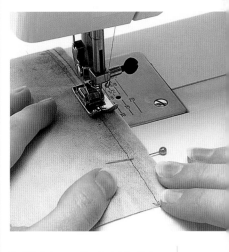

3 Stitch tape with straight stitch on woven fabrics, or with a zigzag stitch on stretch-knit fabrics. ▲

SEAM FINISHES AND EDGES

Different seam finishes are used on different fabric types, or where a decorative finish would improve the appearance. Some of the following seam finishes also finish the seam allowance at the same time.

Bias seams

Bias-cut fabric will stretch more easily because there is more "give" on the bias. To prevent unwanted stretch and to stop seams rippling, hold the fabric in front and behind the presser foot, stretching it slightly as you stitch. The stitching will then relax into a smooth seam once carefully pressed.

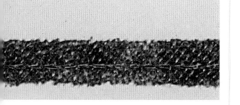

If a bias is to be stitched on a heavier-weight fabric, it might also need stabilizing to prevent sagging and drooping. Add a length of seam tape to the seam line and stitch through all layers.

Knit seams

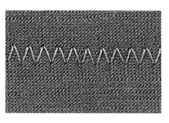

Stretchy fabrics will still need stretch, so they need to have flexible seams. To stitch a flexible seam, choose a stretch stitch or zigzag stitch, stretching the fabric slightly as you sew. ▲ ▼

On areas of knit fabrics that will pull out of shape if they pull out of shape (such as shoulder lines, necklines, etc.), add a strip of fusible stabilizer tape (ease tape) to the seam allowance. Alternatively, with right sides together, stitch a plain seam with seam binding, ribbon, or twill tape along the seam line. ▼

French seam

This is a very neat seam ideal for sheers, lightweight silks, or unlined curtains and blinds, where the reverse will be visible or show through.

1 With the wrong sides together, stitch a ⅜ in (1cm) seam.

2 Trim seam allowance to a scant ⅛ in (3mm). Press.

3 Turn through to right side with stitched line on the fold and press again.

4 Machine stitch ¼ in (6mm) from the fold. Press. ▼

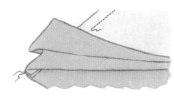

Double-stitched seam

A double-stitched seam is used to provide a strong seam in stretch fabrics, or a narrow seam in sheers and laces. It will also prevent knit fabric edges from curling.

Double-stitched seams are formed by stitching two parallel rows close together, working both in the same direction.

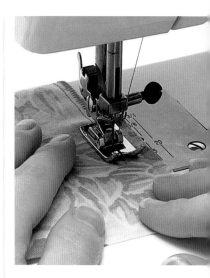

1 Stitch the first row, using straight stitch, along the seam line. ▲

2 Stitch again a scant ⅛ in (3mm) away using either a straight or small zigzag stitch. Trim close to the stitching.

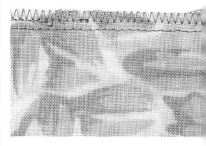

3 On sheers, overcast the raw edges with a small zigzag stitch. Press to set the stitching. ▲

Lapped seam

This seam is used on fabrics that don't ravel or fray such as synthetic suede and leather.

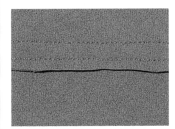

1 Mark the stitching line on the section that will overlap (lap horizontal seams downward and vertical seams away from the center).

2 Trim off the seam allowance on the marked layer of fabric.

3 Lap the fabric over the underneath section, placing the trimmed edge just over the seam line of the under fabric. (If pins will leave holes, use double-sided basting tape that will hold the layers together.)

4 Edge stitch close to the trimmed edge.

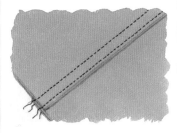

5 Top stitch ¼ in (6mm) from the first row of stitching, catching the seam allowance of the under layer.

Top-stitched seam

This is a plain seam finished with a row of stitching on the right side, which at the same time holds the seam allowances in place. It is a particularly useful seam finish for crease-resistant fabrics or heavyweight fabrics. It also makes the seam more durable.

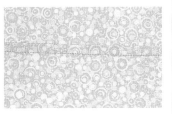

Top stitching can be done in matching thread for a subtle finish, or contrasting thread for a decorative detail. Note, edge stitching is basically the same, but the line of stitching is much closer to the fabric edge—a scant ⅛ in (3mm) as opposed to ¼–⅜ in (6–10mm).

1 Stitch a regular seam, with fabric right sides together. Press and neaten seam allowances.

2 For lightweight fabrics, press seam allowances to one side and then stitch again, working from right side, ¼ in (6mm) from edge, catching seam allowance in place as you stitch.

3 For heavier-weight fabrics, press neatened seam allowances open and double top stitch by stitching on both sides of the seam ⅜ in (10mm) from seam line.

Welt and double-welt seams

This seam is used on fabrics that don't ravel or fray such as synthetic suede and leather.

1 Stitch a regular seam and press seam allowances to one side.

2 Grade the seam allowances by trimming the under edge to ¼ in (6mm) and leaving the upper seam allowance untrimmed.

3 Working from the right side, top stitch ¼ in (6mm) from the seam, catching the untrimmed seam allowance.

4 To make a double-welt seam, add an additional row of edge stitching close to the seam line.

Flat fell seam

This seam finish is often used on sportswear and reversible garments. The seam allowance is sewn on the right side of the fabric, with raw edges tucked under.

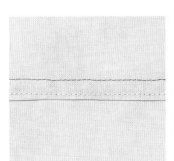

1 Pin fabric with wrong sides together and stitch a regular seam. Press seam allowances to one side.

2 Trim the under seam allowance to a scant ⅛ in (3mm).

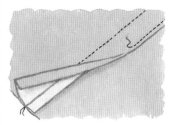

3 Turn under ¼ in (6mm) on the upper seam allowance and baste in place. ▲

4 Edge stitch close to the fold. Press again.

INTERFACINGS AND STABILIZERS

Interfacing is an extra layer applied to the reverse of the fabric in order to add body or enhance firmness or stability in specific areas. Stabilizers are used to hold fabric firm while stitching and are used in densely stitched areas.

There are hundreds of interfacings and stabilizers from which to choose. We look at the most commonly available and the most frequently used.

INTERFACINGS

There is no particular rule on what type to use when, as it depends on the appearance you want to achieve. There are, however, certain areas that must be interfaced to avoid problems when stitching, such as buttonholes, or collars and cuffs, which, without interfacing, would be limp and thus not hang correctly.

The aim of interfacing is to enhance the garment, adding firmness where needed. The weight used is generally the same as the fabric, thus lightweight interfacing with lightweight fabrics or firm heavyweight with heavyweight woolens. On very lightweight, transparent fabrics, the interfacing layer can be made up of an extra layer of the main fabric.

General interfacings can be split into three categories. All three categories include interfacings that can be iron-on (fusible) or sew-in, and come in a variety of weights. **Non-woven**—the traditional home dressmaker selection, made from pressed fibers with a felt-like appearance. **Woven**—fairly new to home dressmakers, these have a fabric grain and are handled in the same manner as fabrics. **Knitted**—again fairly new to home dressmakers, these have two-way stretch so they move like knitted fabrics.

Non-woven

Non-woven interfacing has no "grain" so it can be cut out in any direction which means pattern pieces can be slotted in to achieve an economical layout. ▼

They are available in white and charcoal black and in many different weights from super-light, through to extra-heavy weights. Some include "soft" in their name, others "light," "heavy," or "medium." They can be sew-in or fusible and are suitable for dressmaking and all manner of craft and home furnishings. ▼

Printed interfacings are available with grid lines to follow for patchwork or quilting. There is one designed specifically for use on leather, and home furnishers can select extra firm, almost board-like weights for tiebacks and pelmets, again with pre-printed lines to follow. ▼

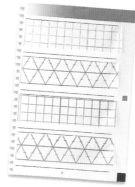

Woven

Woven interfacings have a "grain" line and can be cut on the straight grain or bias in the same manner as fabric. There is more color choice, ranging from cream, skin tone, white, black, or charcoal.

The super-lightweight wovens are ideal when using silks, sheers, and satins. Medium and heavyweight woven fusibles are used on jackets, dresses, and blouses. ▼

Knitted interfacings

These fusible interfacings will stretch with the garment when applied to knit, stretch, or jersey fabrics.

APPLYING INTERFACINGS

Sew-in

Sew-in, as the name suggests, is either hand or machine stitched to the main fabric just within the seam allowance. Use sew-in interfacing on pile fabrics or textured fabrics, which could be damaged by a hot iron.

1 Cut out interfacing to shape of the appropriate pattern piece.

2 Stitch just within the seam allowance.

3 Trim excess interfacing close to stitching. Trim the corners off. ▲

IRON-ON/FUSIBLE

Fusibles can be applied quickly but do need to be fused properly to ensure they remain in place. One side of fusible interfacing is glued and has a slightly raised bobble appearance that may also slightly glisten or shine. Always use a press cloth when applying fusibles. ▶

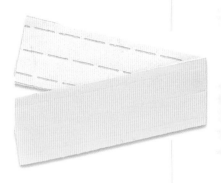

1 Cut fusible interfacing to the size of appropriate pattern pieces and then trim so that it fits just within the stitching line.

2 Place fabric to be interfaced the wrong side up, and interfacing in place, glued side down. Cover with a damp press cloth.

3 Dry press rather than iron. Press the iron onto fused fabric and hold in same position for approximately 10–15 seconds. Lift iron, move to different area, and press down again. Repeat until the whole area has been pressed.

4 Leave fused interfacing to cool completely before continuing to work with it.

TIP *Cover ironing board with a muslin cloth to protect the surface in case any of the glued interfacing overlaps onto the cloth.*

WAISTBANDINGS

These are specialist interfacings designed to be used in specific areas such as waistbands, front bands, or pleats. They are made from non-woven interfacing and are usually fusible.

Slotted banding

The slotted lines down the center and along both edges make them easy to fold and stitch. They are used on waistbands to produce perfect pleats and on front bands as they help to produce a crisp, clean fold. ▼

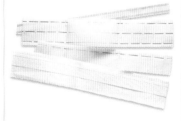

Stiffened banding

These can be the fusible slotted banding with an added strip of stiffened interfacing covering half the banding to produce a roll-resistant waistband or a stand-alone band, approximately 1¼ in (3cm) wide.

APPLYING BANDING TO WAISTBANDS

1 Fuse the slotted banding to the wrong side of the fabric.

2 Fold ¼ in (6mm) of one long edge to the wrong side and press.

3 Right sides together, pin long edge to waistband of garment. Stitch with ⅝ in (15mm) seam allowance so that the stitching falls within the slotted line. Trim seam allowances. Press, with seam allowances toward the waistband.

4 Fold waistbanding at center fold line, right sides together, and sew side edges and overlap end (see Waistbands, page 66).

5 Trim seam allowances, cutting corners at an angle. Turn through to right side.

6 On the wrong side, pin neatened edge of banding over seam, encasing seam allowances. Place pins at right angles so they can be removed as you stitch.

7 Slip stitch in place or, working from right side, stitch in the ditch (see page 37).

To apply banding to pleats, again fuse in place but with the center slotted line on the pleat fold. ▼

HEMMING TAPES

Usually fusible, hemming tapes are a handy alternative to sewing a hem with the added bonus of being absolutely invisible from the right side.

TIP *Make sure you trim hemming tapes before pressing, otherwise they will stick to the iron.*

Web

This is a fine web of glue in a strip approximately ½ in (13mm) wide. It is ideal for narrow hems.

1 To apply, neaten the raw edge of the hem allowance by zigzag stitching or overlocking, then pressing to set the stitches.

2 Fold the hem allowance up to wrong side and then place the web between the layers so that it is ¼ in (6mm) from the neatened edge.

3 Press, using a press cloth, avoiding pressing the neatened edge as it may form a ridge on the right side. The glue web dissolves and sticks the two fabric layers together.

Paper-backed hem tape

Paper-backed hem tape is similar to webbing but it has a paper backing. It is also ideal for narrow hems.

1 Repeat step 1 above.

2 Fold hem allowance up to the wrong side and press. Unfold and place hemming tape, with paper side uppermost, within hem allowance again so it is ¼ in (6mm) below where the neatened edge will sit. Press in place.

3 Peel paper backing off and then refold hem allowance in place. Press again, avoiding the neatened edge (that will leave a ridge). ▼

Blind-hem tape

This is a folded tape which will mimic a blind hem. It is fusible and is ideal for wider hems as the tape itself is 1 in (25mm) wide.

1 Neaten raw edge as step 1 above. Then fold hem allowance up and press.

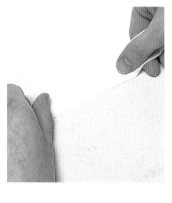

2 Insert blind-hem tape with the opening edge at the top. Fuse in place. ▲

TIP *The actual time to achieve a good bond varies depending on interfacing and fabric weight. It generally takes longer than normal pressing to fuse properly. Always test on a sample first.*

SPECIALIST TAPES

These include bias and edge tapes that are used to add control and stability to specified areas.

Bias tape

This is a fusible curved tape that prevents stretching at armhole edges, necklines, curtains, in fact anything that needs stabilizing on a curve. It comes in charcoal and white. It is fused within the seam allowance in the appropriate areas. ▶

Edge tape

In white only, this is a narrow strip of interfacing that is stitch-reinforced to add stability. It is used in areas that are cut on the bias but which are not supposed to have too much give, for instance on shoulder seams or skirt slits. Again, it is applied to the seam allowance area. ▼

Paper-backed fusible web

This comes in packs and is a double-sided fusible web with paper backing. It is mainly used for positioning appliqué and for mending or repairing.

1 Draw design to be appliquéd in reverse on the paper backing. Cut out roughly.

2 Position on wrong side of appliqué fabric, with fused web to fabric. Press in place and allow to cool before handling again. ▲

3 Cut out accurately and then place on main fabric, with paper side down. Once happy with the position, peel away the paper and fuse into place.

4 Finish appliqué by satin stitching or zigzag stitching around the edges.

Wadding

Fleece, wadding, or batting are all terms used for the dense, soft interfacings that are added for bulk or extra warmth. They are particularly used in craft, patchwork, and quilting projects, and soft furnishings.

They are often described as having extra loft (bulk/density). Again, there are some specialist versions, such as those with pre-printed quilting guide lines or a compressed fleece which is used to provide some heat resistance. ▼

STABILIZERS

Stabilizers or backing interfacings, are used to provide stability when stitching delicate or densely stitched areas. There is a huge range available, from the traditional tear-away stabilizers used when decorative stitching or adding appliqué, to very soft, soluble webs that disintegrate when rubbed with a wet cloth or washed under a cold tap. ▼

TIP *Always use a stabilizer when machine embroidering as the very concentrated number of stitches and thread in a small space can cause fabric to pucker, stretch, or be pulled into the feed dogs.*

Tear-away stabilizer

Available in charcoal black or white, it has a felt-like finish and is quite crisp to handle. Pin it in position to the wrong side of the work being stitched. It will help prevent the fabric puckering as it is stitched and, on fine fabrics, help prevent them being pulled into the feed dogs. After stitching, simply tear away the excess. ▼

Water-soluble stabilizer

This can be used in single or multiple layers. For toweling or other piled fabrics, add one or two layers on top of the work to prevent the stitching disappearing into the pile.

Sandwich very fine fabrics (such as voiles) between layers of soluble stabilizer and machine embroider. Wash away the stabilizers and the embroidery will sit on unpuckered fabric without spoiling the its transparency. ▼

With water-soluble stabilizers, the more water that is applied, the more the stabilizer disappears. To keep a crisp finish, wash gently only. To erase the stabilizer, soak in cold water and then rinse.

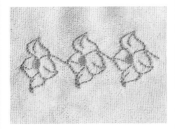

Another useful stabilizer is a self-adhesive embroidery backer. It prevents distortion when working on small areas within an embroidery hoop, such as collars, pockets, etc.

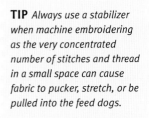

TECHNIQUES FOR SOFT FURNISHINGS

Simple sewing techniques are often the same whether you are sewing for the home or family but there are some soft-furnishing guidelines that make it so much easier.

CURTAINS

Curtains change the appearance of windows, making them look wider, deeper, larger, or smaller. They can also be used (without pulling the draw cords) in other parts of the room to create fabric panels to hide unsightly shelves and storage spaces, as bed canopies, or to cover glass fronted wardrobes.

MEASURING YOUR SPACE

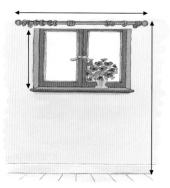

Two basic measurements are needed to determine the overall size—the width at its fullest and the overall length. To ensure both measurements are accurate, choose and position your curtain track prior to measuring.

Width: from the outer edges of the curtain track, which should extend approximately 10 in (25cm) from the window frame.

Length: from the top of the curtain track to the point of the desired length, which can be the sill, radiator, or floor. (If you choose a curtain header tape that will make the drapes start above the curtain track, also add this difference to the total length.)

TIP *If the distance from window to wall (or other vertical obstruction) is less than 7 in (18cm), use a single curtain draped from the clear side instead of two curtains.*

Additional length measurements

First, choose your header tape. This determines the type of gathers or pleats your curtains will have. These tapes can range in width from approximately 1–4 in (25mm–10cm) and this depth needs to be added to the length measurement, as the curtain fabric will be double thickness where the tape is. Also add 3–8 in (8–20cm) for hem allowance. The total length required is: Measurement from top of curtain track to required hem + depth of header tape + 3–8 in (8–20cm) for hems.

OUR EXAMPLE

Our window is 43 in (109cm) wide and the chosen curtain height, from the top of the pole to the skirting board is 89 in (226cm). We are using 3 in (8cm) header tape and want a deep hem, thus we allow 8 in (20cm), which, doubled will make a 4 in (10cm) hem. Thus, the total length is 89 in+3 in header+8 in hem=100 in (228cm+8cm+20cm=254cm).

Drapery (header) tapes

There is a wide range of drapery tapes, from pencil pleats to triple, double, or simply gathered tops. The different pleat styles suit different windows and fabrics. Deep, fully gathered pleats work well on long windows, while narrow-pinch pleats or mini-pleats work well on lightweight, short curtains. The type of header tape also helps determine the width of draping needed to create the right amount of fullness.

Pencil-pleat header tape

Additional width measurements

Having determined the overall length required, you can start calculating the total width and thus the amount of fabric needed to make up the widths. The amount of fabric needed will depend on:
- Fullness of curtains required
- Pattern repeat
- Fabric width

> **TIP** *Some selvages (side edges of fabric) are more tightly woven than the fabric and thus can cause slight puckering. To prevent this, cut the selvages off before joining panels or neatening side edges.*

Fullness of curtains

A good average of curtains is achieved by 2½ times the window width. To get the full width required, you will probably need to join fabric lengths so allow an extra 1 in (25mm) per seam.

Pattern repeat

When a recurring pattern has to be matched, extra fabric is usually required in the length.

Fabric requirement

Multiply the length calculated earlier (plus pattern repeats) by the number of fabric panels required to complete the width. For instance if your chosen window is 43 in (109cm) wide, 2½ times fullness = 107 in or 3 yards (273cm). If your fabric is 45 in (114cm) wide, you will need three lengths of 45 in (114 cm) from which to cut. Sometimes it is necessary to buy three or five lengths to get the total width even though you only need part of one of the lengths. On heavyweight fabrics, cut off the excess and use for tiebacks or pillow trims. On lightweight fabrics, simply have more fullness.

EXAMPLE

To get the total width for our example you need to purchase: 3 x 2¾ yard (254cm) lengths of the 43 in (114cm) wide fabric = 8¼ yards (762cm).

> **TIP** *If you have difficulty working out the amount of fabric needed, take your window measurements to the store and get advice to suit your fabric and curtain header choice.*

CUTTING OUT

Cut the fabric into the desired number of lengths, matching the pattern repeats and, if necessary, cutting one length into two. To match the pattern repeats:

1 With the print facing uppermost, cut the first panel. It may be necessary to square the top edge first.

2 Lay this first panel over the remaining fabric, wrong side of the first panel on top of the right side of the remaining fabric, moving it down from cut edge until the pattern matches. This may mean having some fabric above the top of the first panel. Alternatively, leave the first panel laid flat and lay the remaining fabric alongside, moving it up or down to match the pattern at side edge.

3 Once the pattern repeat is matched, cut along the top and bottom edges by using the first panel as a guide. Repeat for other panels.

MAKING UP UNLINED CURTAINS

1 With right sides together, stitch panels together from bottom to top. Stitch all panels in the same direction. If half panels are used, attach these to the outside edges so that, when closed, the full panels are in the center.

> **TIP** *Use French seams (see All about seams chapter) so that the back looks neat too.*

2 Press seam allowances open and neaten the raw edges on fabrics that fray easily, or on unlined curtains.

3 Neaten side edges by taking a double hem—fold side edge under 1 in (25mm) folding raw edge in again so it meets the first fold. Press and top stitch, again working from bottom to top.

> **TIP** *If using selvages as side seams, clip into the selvage at intervals to prevent the puckering that sometimes occurs because the selvages are more tightly woven than the main fabric grain.*

Hemming

Most professionally made curtains are hand hemmed, after the curtains have hung for a day or two. Lightweight curtains, or those that will "puddle" can be hemmed by machine in advance of adding headers. Before hemming, double check the length, remembering to allow for the header. For heavyweight curtains, neaten the raw hem edge by machine, fold up hem allowance, and pin. Leave to hand stitch later.

Adding headers to curtains

Once the panels are joined, side edges neatened, and the bottom hemmed or prepared for hemming, it is time to add the curtain headers.

1 Turn top curtain edge under the depth of the curtain heading plus ½ in (1cm) and pin heading in place, covering the raw edge. (If the curtain fabric ravels easily, overcast or zigzag stitch the raw edge prior to folding under.) ▼

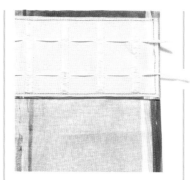

2 Tuck the ends of the tape under, keeping the draw cords free on the side edge, and pin in place. Machine stitch along the top and bottom of the tape, stitching in the same direction both times. Stitch the side edges, keeping the draw cords free on the outer edge. ▲

3 Gather up the tape to achieve the finished width required, gathering from the side edges. ▼

4 You may wish to add a toggle button to the side edge and wind the excess cord around it to keep it neat and out of sight. ▼

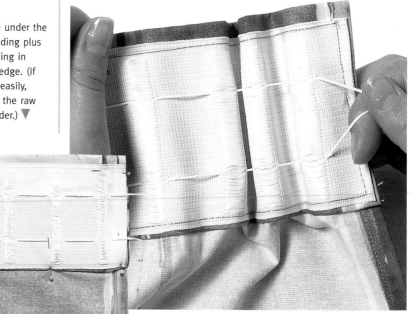

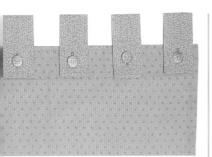

TAB-TOP CURTAINS

These are a popular style of curtains that do not require header tape. Instead, they have tabs, which loop over a curtain pole and are stitched, buttoned, or snapped to the curtain as a decorative finish.

When calculating the curtain length, remember to allow for tab tops. They should hold the top of the curtain above the actual window, so it may be necessary to hang the pole slightly higher than usual.

The width of the tabs will depend on personal preference. However, as a general rule of thumb, the heavier and longer the curtain, the wider each tab can be. The space between tabs will also depend on preference and fabric weight. The heavier the fabric, the closer the tabs should be to prevent sagging between them. As a guide, allow a gap of half the finished tab width between each tab.

MAKING UP

1 Cut each tab approximately 9 in (23cm) long x 5 in (13cm) wide. (Finished tab will be 8 x 2 in [20 x 5cm].)

2 Interface with heavyweight interfacing to produce a crisp, firm finish. ▼

3 Fold the tabs in half lengthwise, right sides together and stitch seam, taking ½ in (13mm) seam allowance.

4 Re-fold so the seam is at center back and then stitch edges of one end together. Trim seam allowances and cut corners at angles. ▲

5 Turn through to right side and then press.

6 If the tab tops are to be buttoned in place, make vertical buttonholes in the center of the finished end, positioned approximately 1 in (25mm) from the end. ▲▼

7 Turn raw edges of open end to inside and press. Top stitch in place. Finish top edge of curtain by double hemming. Press. ▼

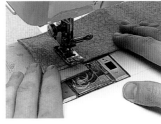

8 Pin tab tops to wrong side of curtain top, with seam of tab facing curtain and with an overlap of at least 1 in (25mm). Position them evenly along the entire width.

9 Stitch in place, stitching a square as shown in diagram. ▼

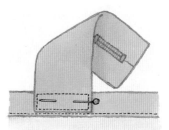

10 Fold tabs to right side of curtain and mark button placement by pinning through bottom edge of buttonholes.

11 Use strong buttonhole thread and stitch buttons with shanks in place. Decorative buttons or self-covered buttons look particularly effective. ▼

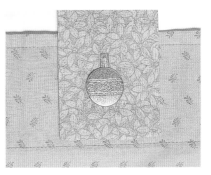

VOILES

Voiles are the new nets and can replace curtains on windows that are not overlooked, or used as additional screening.

A very lightweight, transparent fabric, the fullness of voiles should be three times the window width. Use header tape especially made for voile fabrics, which is clear and lightweight.

Sew a deep hem and add weights to keep voiles hanging evenly, unless they are to puddle on the floor.

Vogue ® Patterns For Living 1596 by Susanna Stratton-Norris

Shapely windows

Curtains can be made for shaped windows and attached with special hook-and-grip header tapes that have an adhesive section and a stitched section. The stitched part is sewn to the curtain edge in the usual manner. The self-adhesive grip tape is applied to the window frame. Gather the curtain to the required width and then press the curtain in place on the grip tape.

Adding linings

Linings will protect the main fabric, add to the density, keeping light and sound out or heat in, help curtains hang, and provide a uniform look from the outside of the house.

There are two types of lining—sewn-in or loose. For loose linings, add a special lining header tape that is attached by hooks to the main curtain but can be taken off when laundering. Loose linings are made up as a normal curtain, with panels stitched together from bottom to top, etc., as detailed above. However, you only need approximately 1½ times the window width in fullness.

Sewn-in linings require almost the same amount as the main fabric—excluding pattern repeats. The total width required is the same as the main fabric, which may also mean cutting a length in half to provide half widths.

Linings can be machine hemmed using a double hem. The lining hem should be shorter than the main curtain. The ideal length is when the lining hem sits just below the inner fold of the curtain hem allowance.

TIP *Before making lined curtains always pre-wash fabric and lining to prevent uneven shrinkage at later laundering.*

ASSEMBLY

Curtain

1 Follow the Cutting out steps 1 and 2 (page 93) to make up the main curtain fabric. Turn side edges under, press and pin, but do not stitch at this point.

2 Turn up and pin hem allowance on curtain length, and then turn top edge down a distance equal to the header tape plus ½ in (13mm). Tuck raw edge under. Re-measure to check finished length, from folded hem edge to folded top. If necessary, cut off excess fabric from top edge.

Lining

3 Cut and piece the lining, stitching panels, right sides together, from bottom to top.

4 Make a double hem in bottom edge, turning fabric under 2 in (5cm) and then again 2 in (5cm) so that raw edge meets first fold. Press and top stitch in place. ▼

Attach lining

5 With curtain wrong side up, lay lining right side up over the curtain, placing it so the bottom of the lining hem is at least 1 in (25mm) from the hem edge.

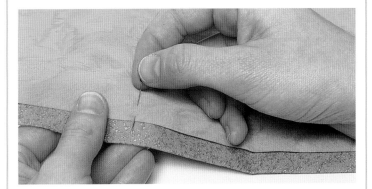

6 Pin through all thicknesses at the hem allowances and then working from center and bottom, smooth lining over curtain, pressing and pinning at intervals to hold layers together. ▲

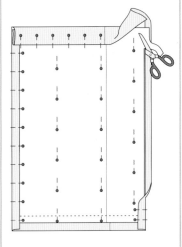

7 If necessary trim the top of the lining so it is in line with curtain top edge, then unpin curtain top and tuck lining under. Re-pin. ▲

8 Repeat for side edges, trimming lining so it matches side edge of curtain, then unpinning curtain sides and tucking raw edge of lining in. Re-pin.

9 Finish side edges by top stitching, hand stitching, or fusing with hemming tape.

10 Add header tape following step 1–4 of unlined curtains, adding headers.

11 Allow to hang for at least 24 hours before hemming.

TIP *If both lining and curtain have panels, offset the lining slightly, keeping the seams parallel but ½ in (13mm) apart to reduce bulk.*

Weights

The draping of any curtains, sheers, or nets is significantly improved if the hems are weighted. Weights are applied as the hem is finished and may be round discs sewn to the seam ends or a series of small lead weights held together in a net tape. This is threaded into the hem allowance and anchored at either end, or on narrow hems can be laid along the hem fold line as it is folded up. The length of tape required is the same as the total flat width of the curtain hem.

TIP *Freshen up and straighten the folds of existing curtains using a steam iron. Gently tug folds at the hem as suggested above whilst spraying steam from a short distance. Once dry, tie in position as in step 3.*

PERFECTLY DRAPED

Once curtains have been hung, they can be trained to hold their position by following these steps:

1 Hold the bottom hem in line with the pleat at the top and gently tug at the hem, gripping in place with a bulldog clip. Then run your hand down the length of the curtain along the natural fold created. Repeat across the width of the curtain.

2 On curtains that hang below the poles (such as tab tops), push the space between each tab/pleat backward as you gently push the curtains to the side. If the curtain heading covers the track, pull the spaces between pleats forward to stand proud of the track.

3 Hold the folds in position by tying a spare length of fabric around the entire curtain at top, middle and hem edge. Leave overnight to "train" the folds.

Roman blinds

Of the many types of blind styles, Roman blinds are probably the easiest to make and the most common. Mounted on a board, attached to the top of the window, they can have a weighted hem or unweighted shaped hem. They are raised and lowered by a system of tapes, cords, and rods at the back of the blind.

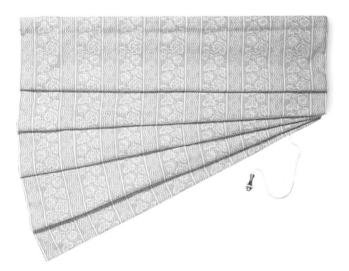

As blinds need to fit the window snugly, the first task is to measure the window space accurately—usually within the recess. If it is to fit outside the recess, remember to measure approximately 3 in (8cm) beyond the window to ensure the blind fully covers the recess and prevents light seeping in.

TIP For large windows, consider 2–3 blinds to fill the gap, dividing the widths by the window structure.

TIP To help determine the amount of tape and cording required, sketch out the window shape and size and mark up spacing and number of rows of tape.

MEASURING FOR BLINDS

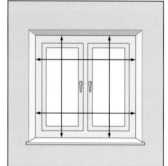

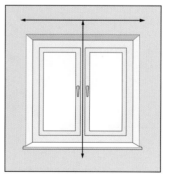

1 Measure from top to bottom twice across the window width (inside or outside the recess).

2 Measure from side to side twice (taking into account tiling on lower half of the window space).

MATERIALS NEEDED

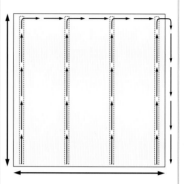

Mounting Board—2 x 1 in wide (5cm x 25mm) cut ½ in (13mm) shorter than the finished width of the blind (or 6 in [15 cm] larger for blinds mounted outside the recess).

Roman blind tape—to determine the amount needed, multiply the finished length of the blind by the number of rows of tape (one for each side and others at intervals of 8–10 in [20–25cm] across the blind).

Cording—enough to thread up each row of tape plus run along the top and down the side (as an estimate, double the tape length required).

Hook-and-loop tape—the window width less ½ in (13mm). This is to attach the blind to the mounting board (preferably sew-and-stick variety).

Screw eyelets—to thread cord through at the top of each row of tape.

Awning cleat and weighted shade pull

Fabric requirements

To determine fabric needed, take the measurements of the window recess and add 5 in (13cm) seam allowances/hems to the width and 9 in (23cm) to the length.

• Remember to allow extra if piecing is required to get the full width, or if pattern repeats are applicable (see Curtains, page 92 to recap on pattern repeats/paneling).

• Cut the fabric to size.

ASSEMBLING

1 Lay the fabric out flat, wrong side uppermost. Turn under one side edge and pin a double hem by turning under 1¼ in (3cm)

and then again to encase raw edge. Repeat for the other side. Press in place.

2 Turn a double hem of 2½ in (6.5cm) on bottom and 2 in (5cm) on top edge. Pin and press. ▼

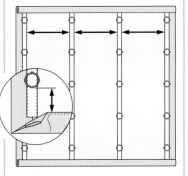

3 Pin the rows of ring tape in place just inside the side edges and then evenly spaced at intervals, running parallel to side edges. (Space rows 8–10 in [20–25cm] apart.) Position so the bottom ring in the tape is 3 in (8cm) from the top of the lower hem—allowing at least 1 in (25mm) of tape to tuck under the hem allowance at both ends.

4 Pinning the hem allowance top and bottom out of the way, machine stitch, along both long edges, each row of tape. Fold back the hem allowance. Stitch each line in the same direction to prevent distortion or puckering.

5 Fold lower hem allowances back in place and top stitch. If desired, add trimmings to the hem edge.

6 Unfold the first fold of the top hem allowance and position hook-and-loop fastener along the length approximately ¼ in (6mm) from top. Machine stitch along both long edges, again working in the same direction each time, and stitching to hem allowance only.

7 Re-fold the hem allowance and top stitch in place.

8 If using a weighted hem, slot the lattice strip or weighted board through the lower hem.

MOUNTING AND CORDING

1 Carefully line up the blind with mounting board and position corresponding hook tape on the face of the board. If necessary, staple in place. Attach blind. ▼

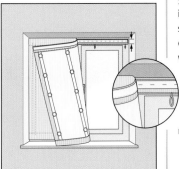

2 Turn the blind face down on a flat surface and then attach the screw eyelets to the underside of the board, lining them up with the rows of tape.

3 Tie a cord length at the bottom of each ring tape, and thread up through the rings then across the

top to one corner, leaving a tail the length of the blind. Cord all tapes in the same manner, taking them across the top to the same side each time.

4 Attach the mount board to the window recess (using angle irons or screws) and then adjust the cords so that the tension of each is equal. ▼

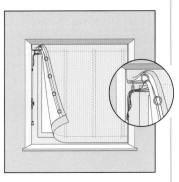

5 Tie all cords securely together in a knot at the upper corner and seal with glue. Trim away all but one cord length and attach the weighted blind pull (it is this one that will be used to lower/raise the blind).

6 Finish with a cleat at the side midway down the window frame.

TIP *If attaching the mount board is tricky, pull up the blind and anchor cords temporarily until board is mounted. Then release cords and adjust as above.*

Quick pillows and tiebacks

Add a new set of pillows and tiebacks to your room décor and you've got a refreshing new look. Here you'll find tips to make quick pillows with envelope backs as well as banana-shaped tiebacks. Add some trimmings for a professional finishing touch.

QUICK PILLOWS

Pillow pads come ready made in standard sizes such as small—12 in (30cm), medium—16 in (40cm), and large—20 in (50cm), so all you need is fabric to cover them and trims to finish them.

1 The easiest, removable pillow cover is the square envelope-backed cover. This is made from one full size front piece and two backs, cut at two-third size to overlap. The cover front can be cut the same size as the pillow pad so it is nice and plump when stuffed. As an example, for a 16 in (40cm) pillow pad, cut one fabric section 16 in square (40cm square) and two back pieces, 16 x 11 in (40 x 28cm).

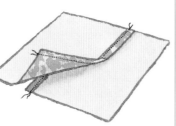

2 Neaten one of the short edges of the back sections by double hemming—turning the fabric to wrong side ³⁄₈ in (10mm) and again so the raw edge meets first fold. ▲

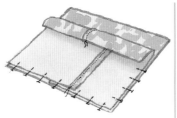

3 Then pin backs to front, right sides together with raw edges matching and the neatened edges of the back pieces overlapping. ▲

4 Machine stitch all round, taking a ¼ in (6mm) seam allowance. Press and trim seam allowances, cutting corners at an angle. Turn through and press again before inserting pillow pad.

5 If desired, add snap fasteners to keep overlap in position.

DECORATION

A pillow can be turned from a plain accessory into a beautifully decorative asset by adding different finishing touches. Here are a few ideas:

Add appliqué

Before stitching the pillow pieces together, appliqué the front panel with colors or motifs to match the room décor. First interface the wrong side of the panel or pin tearaway stabilizer to the back. Apply the motif (see Appliqué in Finishing touches, page 104) and then sew cover sections together as above.

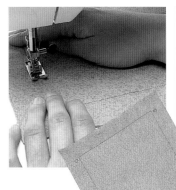

Flanged pillows

Still using the envelope design, make flanged pillow covers by cutting the pieces 3 in (8cm) larger than the pad. Thus, for a 16 in (40cm) pad, the front will be 19 in (48cm) square and the backs 19 x 13 in (48 x 33cm). Sew together as before and then turn through. Make the flange by top stitching 1 in (25mm) from edges all around. Add a row of decorative stitching within the flange if desired.

Trimmed pillows

Trimming can be added to the front cover before it is attached to the backs, to the outside by hand once the cover is sewn, or in-seam. Trims to add on top include ric-rac, ribbon, lace, or braid. Trims to stitch in-seam include those with one decorative edge, beaded trims, or piping (for details of adding trims, turn to Finishing touches, page 104).

Add decorative trim to the right side of front section, 1¼ in (3cm) from edge. For trims stitched in-seam, again lay on front cover, so the tape edge is in line with pillow-cover raw edge. Machine stitch in place. Add neatened back panels as before, sandwiching the trim. Stitch as close to beading as possible, using a zipper foot. Turn through as before.

Alternative shapes and sizes

Covers for other pillow shapes can be stitched just as easily. Simply cut the shape by using the pad as a template. If adding a zipper to close the cover, add ¾ in (2cm) seam allowance along the edge to be zipped.

• For covers that will not be removed, simply cut two pieces the same size, sew together as before but leaving a gap of at least 8 in (20cm) (for turning and inserting pad).

• Add buttons to the centers of round pillows, using a strong buttonhole twist thread to stitch in place.

• Add tassels to corners of plain pillows and you've got a great look in minutes. Hand stitch them on, using thread to match pillow fabric.

• Make your own pillow pads by sewing together three sides of two panels of fabric, wrong sides together (whatever size or shape you desire). Stuff with batting and stitch remaining side together. There is no need to turn the pad through as it will be inside the cover anyway.

TIEBACKS

Making matching tiebacks is a good way to finish off the décor. The banana shape is easy to draw and make. As with pillow covers, you can add trims and piping and, again, these would be added before stitching front and back sections together.

To make a simple banana-shaped tieback, you will need approximately ¾ yd (69cm) of main fabric, ½ yd (50cm) of heavyweight fusible interfacing, four rings, and two hooks.

1 Draw a half banana shape on paper to use as a template, following our diagram. ▲

2 Place the template on fabric that has been folded, right sides together, matching the straight edge of template with the fold.

3 For each tieback cut out two fabric pieces—for back and front.

4 Trim template by ⅝ in (15mm) all around and cut out fusible interfacing (matching weight of interfacing to fabric weight).

5 Apply interfacing with the iron and, once cooled, pin tieback sections, right sides together.

6 Stitch, taking ⅝ in (15mm) seam allowance and leaving a turning gap in the bottom edge.

7 Clip and notch seam allowance (leaving turning gap seam allowance untrimmed). Turn through and press.

8 Slip stitch opening and add rings to ends.

Piped tieback

Piping gives the tieback a crisp neat finish and can look particularly effective if the piping is in a contrasting color that picks up colors from the curtains.

1 Allow 2 yards (2m) of ¼ in (6mm) wide piping.

2 Apply piping to right side of one section as described in Piping, Finishing touches, page 106 before stitching front and back sections together. ▼

chapter three

SPECIAL SEWING TECHNIQUES

Finishing touches

Couture techniques

Sewing with special fabrics

Creative sewing

FINISHING TOUCHES

Add creative embellishments to clothes, drapes, and pillows to make a statement of stylish individualism.

APPLIQUÉ

An appliqué is a fabric design applied on to a base fabric. It can be a simple colored block, a pattern, or a combination of fabrics creating a picture. You can also purchase ready-made appliqué designs.

The technique is used to add a finishing touch to soft furnishings, accessories, or children's clothing. There are four main types of appliqué: plain, raw-edge, shadow, and reverse.

Steps to sew

1 Appliqués are usually stitched with a very narrow zigzag or satin stitch, or with a blanket stitch (if the appliqué fabric doesn't ravel easily). Use a satin stitch/appliqué-presser foot, which has a tiny groove in the bottom that slips smoothly over the concentrated row of stitches.

2 Anchor the appliqué in position prior to stitching by bonding it to the main fabric using either double-sided fusible web or a light application of fabric glue.

3 If adding appliqué to lightweight fabrics, place a piece of tear-away stabilizer under the work for added stability. (This is torn away once the stitching is complete but will prevent the fabric being pulled when it is being stitched.)

Plain appliqué

Plain appliqué is the most frequently used technique and is the method used to add motifs or to create pictures on clothing and soft furnishings. (For raw edge, shadow, reverse, and mola appliqué turn to Creative sewing, page 132).

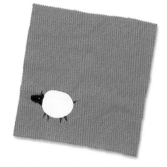

1 Apply paper-backed, double-sided fusible web to wrong side of the appliqué fabric or motif. Draw around the desired design on the paper backing and then cut out accurately, shown below left. (If using lettering or

numbers, remember to draw back to front so when turned to right side, they will be correct.) ▼

2 Position the appliqué the right way up on main fabric and, once satisfied with positioning, remove paper backing and fuse in place.

3 Using a satin stitch/appliqué foot and set machine for satin stitch or narrow zigzag, width 3, length 0.45. Place the appliqué under foot, so the right swing of needle will be off the edge of the appliqué. ▼

TIP *Test stitch a sample of fabric with the same number of layers and interfacing.*

4 Stitch slowly to control direction and ensure smooth edges. When working curves or corners, stop with needle down in the right-hand position so it is in the main fabric for outward curves. Lift presser foot to pivot fabric slightly before continuing. For inside curves, stop with the needle in the appliqué, then raise presser foot, pivot, and continue as before.

ADDING TRIMS, BRAIDS, AND CORDS

Simply adding a trim, braid, cord, or piping can turn a very plain pillow into a decorative accessory that co-ordinates with your room décor. Trims with neatened edges can be applied by hand to finished projects. Trims on base tape, such as beaded trims or piping, need to be added before seams are sewn.

Applying finished trims

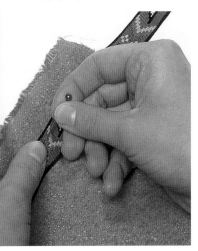

1 Lay the trims on the right side of the pillow cover, curtain, or dress, approximately 1 in (25mm) from the hem edge. Once happy with positioning, pin in place. ▲

2 For trims over ¼ in (6mm) wide, machine stitch down both long edges, working in the same direction each time. For trims under ¼ in (6mm), machine stitch down the center.

Mitering trims

When applying trims, braids, or bindings, it may be necessary to work around corners. To achieve a crisp, professional-looking result, fabric needs to be mitered. Whether stitching flat trims or those with fancy edges, the basic technique is the same.

1 Pin the trim in place and top stitch both edges, ending stitching on the seam line at corner. ▼

2 Fold the trim back upon itself and press. Holding this fold, fold the trim again, this time at right angles to the first line of trim so that the edge is along the next placement line. Press. ▼

3 Undo the second fold so the trim is just folded back on itself. Stitch along the diagonal crease through all layers. ▼

4 Turn the trim back down the diagonal line of stitching and press. Continue top stitching both edges. ▼

In-seam trims

These are trims with a base tape that is stitched within seam allowance so only the dangling trim hangs loose.

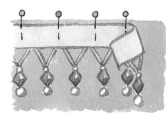

1 Pin the trim to the right side of the main fabric, with tape edge matching the fabric raw edge. ▲▼

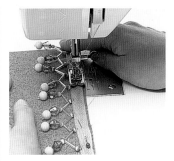

2 Machine stitch in place, ¼ in (6mm) from edge. ▲

3 Place second layer of fabric over trimmed fabric, right sides together, sandwiching the trim between them.

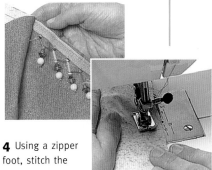

4 Using a zipper foot, stitch the seam, working as close to the beading as possible, without catching dangling beads. ▲

5 Clip the seam allowances of both fabrics and trim tape. Turn to the right side.

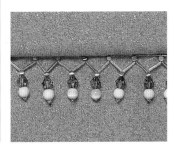

PIPING

Piping is a raised cord edging applied to soft furnishing and some tailored garments. It can be decorative cord or a plain cord covered with fabric. Piping is applied following steps 1–5 of the in-seam trim method.

Fabric-covered piping

1 Cut strips of bias-cut fabric approximately 1 in (25mm) wide. Join strips together if necessary to get one continuous strip.

2 Fold the strips in half lengthways, wrong sides together, and sandwich plain cord in the fold. ▲

3 Machine stitch folded fabric, encasing the cord. ▲

4 Follow steps 1–5 on page 105 to apply.

BIAS BINDING

Bias binding is so called because it is a binding made from strips of fabric that have been cut on the bias. It can be used to neaten and encase raw edges, and provide a decorative trim. It is often found on garment necklines, armholes, or on edge-to-edge jackets, as

TIP *The lighter the fabric being bound, the narrower the binding tape can be. Heavier fabrics require wider binding.*

TIP *If making your own bias binding, work on an ironing board, following the instructions that come with the binding tape maker. Press with a hot iron as the folded fabric comes out of the tape maker in order to set the folds in place.*

well as on craft projects such as tablecloths, pillows, and tiebacks. It is ideal on reversible garments such as jackets, vests, or capes, or when using translucent fabrics where a facing would show through.

Bias binding can be purchased ready made in a variety of widths and different fabric finishes, or can be made at home using a bias tape maker. There are different sizes of these available to make wide or narrow binding. The bias binding is formed by a strip that has the side edges folded equally to the center on the wrong side. ▼

Another type of bias tape is foldover braid. This is simply folded in two, just off center so that one edge is wider than the other.

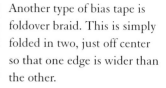

Applying bias binding

1 Pin opened-out binding, right side to right side of fabric edge.

2 Machine stitch binding in place, stitching along the crease of the fold line nearest to the raw edges. ▼

4 Fold binding over to wrong side, encasing the raw edges. Pin folded edge over previous stitching line.

3 Trim seam allowances to the bare minimum (so that when the binding is folded over, the raw edges will be encased and the second folded edge is in line with the stitched edge). Clip and notch at the curves in the usual manner.

5 Slip stitch folded binding in place. (Alternatively, machine stitch from the right side, stitching "in-the-ditch" whilst catching the underside in place [see page 37]. ▼

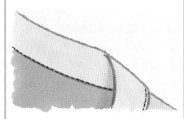

Joining ends

When binding a project where the binding ends will meet, follow these steps:

1 Turn under raw edge of one short end of the binding and press to hold.

2 Start with the folded end of the binding at an inconspicuous area (side seam, under arm, etc.) and proceed as steps 1–3 above.

3 Lap the unpressed end over the pressed end. (Once binding is folded over, pressed edge will be uppermost.)

Binding inside corners

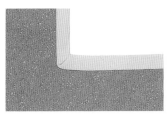

1 To bind an inside corner, first reinforce stitch the corner at the seam line by stitching ½ in (13mm) either side of the corner, using small machine stitches.

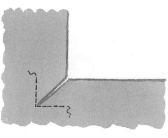

2 Clip the corner close to the stitches. ▲

3 Stitch binding to right side as step 2 of Applying bias binding, stitching until the corner is reached. With needle down, raise presser foot and spread the fabric open at the clipped corner, so it is almost a straight line. ▼

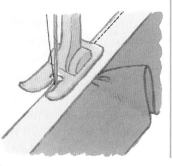

4 Lower the presser foot and continue to apply binding.

5 Press seam allowances toward the binding to form a diagonal of fabric at corner. ▼

6 Turn binding to inside, encasing raw edges, and forming another diagonal fold on the inside. Finish the binding as step 5 of Applying bias binding above, slip stitching the corner folds in place.

GIMPING AND COUCHING

Add a raised surface detail to soft furnishings or garments by couching or gimping cord, braids, and ribbons. The term gimping (also known as couching in Europe) describes the method of fixing the trim in place. Plain cords are often attached by satin stitching over

them. Fancy trims will be zigzagged in position so the trim is still visible. In both methods, the trim is not actually stitched at all. Use flexible cords for scrolls, curves, and corners.

1 Mark a placement line on the right side of the fabric.

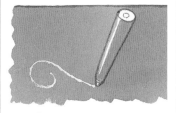

2 Pin trim or cord in place, pinning frequently around curves. Select satin stitch (or very close zigzag stitch) and thread color to match fabric or trim (depending on personal preferences). For fancy trims, a simple zigzag stitch will suffice.

3 Position at start, so that needle will penetrate fabric just to the left or right of the trim (as close as possible without stitching through the trim itself). Work one or two stitches very slowly, checking to see that the needle swings over the cord, penetrating either side as close as possible. If the stitch length is too long, and the stitches are not close to the cord, reduce the stitch length.

4 Continue stitching over the cord, working slowly at the curves and corners. ▲

> **TIP** Before gimping on a project, try a test piece first.

GIMPING IDEAS

• Add a naval feel to collars and cuffs by couching two rows of cord in position with gold thread.

• For a nautical look to cushions, simply couch down white cord or yarn using a zigzag stitch.

• Add decorative trims to plain garments along pocket edges, hemlines, or on cushion panels.

> **TIP** Use a gimping/cording presser foot (available for most makes of sewing machine), which has grooves in the base of the foot through which the cord is fed. This saves pinning cord in place prior to stitching.

DECORATIVE TOP STITCHING

Top stitching is done quite literally on the top of a project. Frequently stitched in a contrast color, it can be a row of straight stitching, decorative stitches, multi-rows, etc. Edge stitching is very similar, but is stitched closer to the edge and usually in a matching thread color.

Preparing to top stitch

1 Press the edge to be stitched, ensuring the seam lines are on the edge or very slightly to the underside (if applicable).

2 Use a thicker-than-normal needle—size 12–14 (80–90) and longer stitch length (3–3.5mm).

3 Stitch a single row at least ⅜–⅝ in (10–15mm) from edge.

4 If stitching more than one row, stitch all the rows in the same direction.

5 Try top stitching ideas on test pieces using same number of layers, interfacings, etc.

TOP STITCHING IDEAS

• Use a twin needle (two needles on one shank) and stitch two parallel rows at once. Use different colored threads for each needle. ▲

> **TIP** If your machine doesn't have two thread spindles, wind some thread onto a bobbin and place it above the thread on the spindle.

• Use some of the decorative stitches available on your machine. Try a combination of stitches. ▼

• Add one row in a contrasting color. ▼

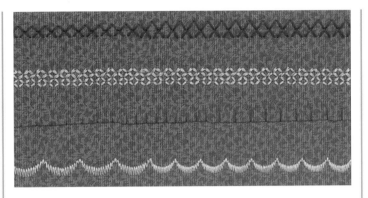

DECORATIVE MACHINE EMBROIDERY

Many of today's modern machines have the ability to machine embroider a number of designs as well as decorative stitches. Some stitches are used to mimic a hand-stitched finish—such as blanket stitch, honeycomb stitch, or cross stitch. Others are traditionally used as decorative finishes, such as shell stitch, scallop stitch, or other satin stitch (very close to zigzag stitch) combinations.

Stitching with machine embroidery

1 If stitching a densely embroidered pattern such as a flower or motif, use bobbin fill in the bobbin rather than regular thread (bobbin fill is a finer thread, which reduces the bulk of thread in a concentrated area). It is normally available in white or black. Use white for light fabrics and black for dark fabrics.

2 For heavily stitched areas, add a layer of stabilizer to the back of the work and place in an embroidery hoop to keep the fabric taut and to prevent it from puckering and pulling. ▼

Stabilizers

The term stabilizer is used to describe any method of adding stability to work while it is being stitched. There are a number of types of stabilizer available, from those that are torn away once the seam or pattern is stitched, to others that are soluble. Plain tissue paper can also be used to stabilize seam areas on slippery fabrics or very fine fabrics. Once the seam is stitched, simply tear the tissue away.

3 Use a chalk pencil or vanishing marker to draw placement lines for rows of decorative stitching. Stitch all rows in the same direction.

4 Press, with a press cloth, from the back of the work so stitches are not flattened.

5 If using decorative thread or metallic thread, use a large-eyed needle or one coated with teflon.

6 Fix stitch at the end of embroidery or take thread tails through to back of work. Tie off and then weave thread ends between stitching, pull taut before cutting so thread will disappear within stitching when released.

DECORATIVE MACHINE EMBROIDERY IDEAS

• Add a motif to a pocket or decorative rows to jacket fronts, collars, and cuffs.

• Stitch a row of motifs along a hemline.

• Use a combination of decorative stitches to decorate a plain pillow panel or tieback.

COUTURE TECHNIQUES

The saying "little things make a big difference" is certainly true of home sewing. Many couture techniques are concerned with finishing the inside of a garment—the hidden details.

UNDERLININGS AND LININGS

Well-tailored garments are lined to help them hang properly, to give extra body and stability, as well as to hide seams and interfacings. Lining fabrics are usually tightly woven, lightweight, and must be compatible with the main fabric in terms of laundry care.

Where possible, match lining color to main fabric color or choose a neutral shade.

The underlining is either sandwiched between the wrong side of main fabric and lining as another layer, or simply sewn as one with the main fabric—so the wrong sides of lining and fabric are placed together before seams are stitched in the normal manner.

A loose lining has nearly all the same pieces as the main garment (excluding facings, waistbands, collars, and cuffs). These are stitched together before being joined to main garment at neck and side edges. Nowadays linings can be added by machine, making them much quicker to complete.

Underlinings

1 Cut underlining pieces from the same pattern pieces as the main garment sections (excluding waistbands, facings, and cuffs).

2 Transfer any pattern markings to the right side of the underlining sections and then pin linings to main fabric, wrong sides together, matching the raw edges.

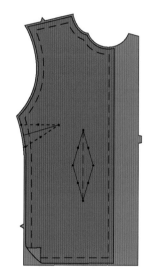

3 Baste underlining to main fabric approximately ½ in (13mm) from edges and through center of darts, pocket placements etc. ▲

4 Construct garment following pattern instructions, treating the two layers as one.

Hemming

1 Turn hem allowance of both layers up along hem fold line. Gently press. Trim main fabric evenly all around if necessary.

2 Unfold and trim away hem part of lining along the fold line. ▲

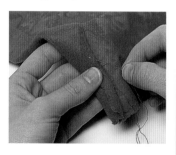

3 Neaten the raw edge of main fabric hem edge and then refold along the fold line. Hand blind stitch in place, catching the lining in stitching. ▲

Slip or loose lining

Loose linings can be added to dresses, pants, and jackets.

1 Cut lining pieces from the same pattern pieces as main garment (unless the pattern provides separate tissue pieces). Exclude waistbands, facings, collars, and cuffs.

2 Treat the lining in the same manner as the main garment, making it up following instructions. Leave any openings for zippers about 1 in (25mm) longer than the main garment.

Dresses and pants

1 Sew the body of garment and lining and then pin lining to garment, wrong sides together, pinning at neckline and armhole edges on dresses or tops, and at waistline on pants. ▲

2 Match darts, seams, centers, notches, and any raw edges.

3 Baste then machine stitch lining and main garment together along neckline, armhole edges, or the waistline on pants.

4 At zipper placement, turn raw edge of lining under and slip stitch along the zipper tape. ▲

5 Finish neckline and armholes with facings so that they enclose the raw edges (see Facings and bands, page 68). Finish waistline with waistband (see Waistbands, page 66).

6 Hem main garment, using a blind hem stitch. Then turn lining hem edge to inside, so the lining hem just sits over the stitched edge of the jacket hem allowance. Slip stitch lining to main hem allowance.

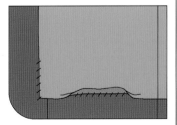

Jackets

Jacket linings need to have pleats and wearing ease wherever the garment needs to give with the movement of the body. This includes center back, bust area, and hems of sleeves and garment. If separate lining pieces are not provided in the pattern, adjust tissue pieces by adding ½–1 in (13–25mm) for a pleat from neck to hem at center back.

1 Attach the under collar to jacket but not upper collar or facings. Remember to pleat lining at center back, catching just the pleat at the top edge.

2 Sew upper collar and jacket facings together following pattern instructions, then sew the combined piece, right sides together to the lining, at sides and across neckline. Begin and end seam approximately 5 in (12.5cm) from lower side edges.

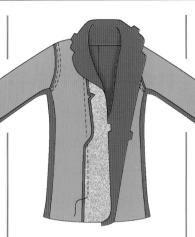

Note you are sewing the inside edges of facings to linings that on an unlined jacket would be neatened. ▲

3 With right sides together, pin and baste facings/upper collar to jacket body, matching all notches and markings. Machine stitch and then trim and grade seam allowances (see All about seams, Reducing bulk, page 84). ▼

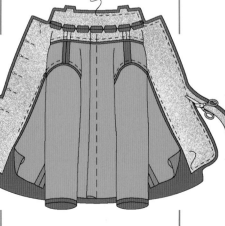

4 Press carefully and then turn right side out.

5 Hem as step 6 above.

Using weights to hold shape

Hem weights are used to hold garments in shape or to prevent embarrassing moments if, for example, the wind catches a skirt. This couture finish adds a professional touch to jackets, coats, smart dresses, and skirts. There are different types of weight—those hidden inside hem allowances and those that form part of the design. Both types are hand sewn in place and should be removed before dry cleaning to prevent unsightly ridges being pressed in by accident.

CHAIN WEIGHTS

These are usually visible and are used to control the drape of a jacket, cardigan, or coat and help keep the hemline level when the garment is worn. Chain weights are usually sewn around the entire hem, starting and finishing at the front opening. However, if a jacket or coat has heavy buttons, the weight can be used in the back hem allowance only, in order to provide a counterbalance.

• The position of the hem weight depends mainly on personal preference. For unlined jackets and coats, it can be stitched on the hem allowance, either just below the hem stitching or approximately ¼ in (6mm) from the edge.

• For lined garments, the chain weight can be placed under the lining hem but on top of the hem allowance of the main garment.

> **TIP** *If chain weight is not available, use costume jewelry chains instead.*

• Apply weights after the jacket has been fully pressed. If the garment has to be pressed once the weight is in position, press carefully to avoid leaving an unsightly ridge.

• As most patterns will not add weights among the notions, the amount needed has to be calculated.

• For all-round weight, measure the hem edge from the center front round to the other center front. Add 2–3 in (5–8cm for ease).

• For the back hem weight only, measure from side seam to side seam. Add 1–2 in (25mm–5cm) for ease.

> **TIP** *If buying the chain at the same time as other notions, check the pattern envelope for finished garment measurements to determine how much chain weight is needed.*

Applying chain weight

1 Using a single strand of hand-sewing thread, catch stitch every third or fourth link to hem allowance, working along the top of the chain. ▲

2 Repeat along the bottom of the chain.

> **TIP** *Wax the thread before stitching to prevent tangles.*

DRAPERY WEIGHTS

Lead discs, also know as penny or drapery weights are ideal for smart jackets, skirts, and draped neck edges. They can be round or square and have stitching holes. Lead weights can be cut smaller, but do remember to hammer flat edges to prevent ridges.

When used in hems, they are inserted in the hem allowance at front jacket edges, back edges and occasionally side seams. To hold draped neckline in place, they can be enclosed in a separate pouch made from lightweight fabric, which is then hand stitched to the facing.

Applying drapery weights

1 Before finishing the hem, place weights in the seam allowance of the hem allowance at front edges, back edges, and if desired, side seams. Position them approximately ¼ in (6mm) up from the hem-fold line.

2 Hand stitch in place.

3 For draped necklines, make a pouch from a rectangle of lining fabric approximately 4 x 3 in (10 x 8cm). Fold it in half and stitch at either side before turning through. Insert a drapery weight before tucking raw edges of pouch to the inside and slip stitching the opening.

4 Attach the pouch to the garment so the weight holds the drape in place. ▼

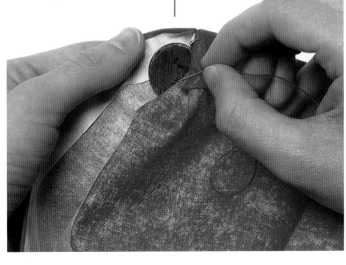

LEAD-WEIGHT TAPES

This type of weighted tape is really a series of little sausage-shaped lead weights encased in a tape. They are used to weight entire hems invisibly and are inserted within the hem allowance. Lead-weight tape is also used to weight hems of voile curtains and lightweight drapes.

Applying lead weight tapes

1 Turn up the hem allowance in the normal manner, leaving a small gap through which to feed the tape.

2 Using a large safety pin, feed the weighted tape through the folded hem allowance, letting it sit in the fold. ▲

3 Catch the stitch at either end of the hem, just inside the hem allowance.

INSERTING LACE PANELS

A special couture finish is achieved by inserting lace or other transparent panels as decorative design details. These panels can be added to yokes, at waistlines, on sleeves, etc., and are sewn over the fabric, which is then cut away from behind the trim.

1 Decide on the positioning by placing the lace trim on the right side. Once satisfied with positioning, pin in place so the trim is right side up (wrong side facing the right side of garment).

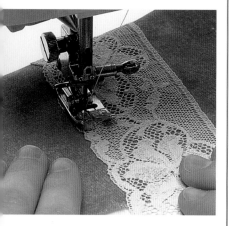

2 Machine stitch along both long edges through all thicknesses. If working with a scalloped lace edge, stitch just within the curves so the scalloped edging remains free. ▲

3 Turn garment to wrong side and carefully cut away the fabric within the two rows of stitching, leaving a ¼ in (6mm) seam allowance along the edges. ▲

4 Press seam allowance toward the fabric along stitching lines.

5 Turn work to the right side again and then edge stitch close to folded edges of fabric, through all layers. Stitch in the same direction as before. If working with scallop-edge lace, fold lace back and edge stitch main fabric and seam allowances only, keeping the scallop edge free. ▼

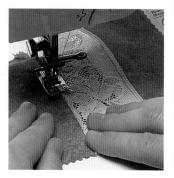

6 Finish by turning to the wrong side again and trimming the seam allowances as close to this second row of stitching as possible. ▼

TIP *If adding lace panels from seam to seam, insert the panel before stitching side or sleeve seams, so the side edges are encased within the seam allowance.*

FASTENINGS

There are a number of different methods of fastening two fabric sections together. These include zippers and buttons with buttonholes, which have already been covered, as well as button loops, bound buttonholes, hooks, eyes, snaps, and hook-and-loop fasteners.

BUTTON LOOPS

Button loops are used instead of buttonholes as decorative details, and are used on edge-to-edge garments and cuffs. They are often combined with round buttons, shaped buttons, or toggles, which are more difficult to slip through buttonholes. The loops can be made of bias strips of the main fabric, from braid or cording, or can be purchased as ready-made loops, evenly spaced on a ⅝ in (15mm) wide tape.

BUTTON LOOPS ON TAPE

Normally white, these are used for quick easy rows of loops. They are applied in the same manner as beaded trims, with the tape sandwiched between the main fabric and the facing/lining. Stitch a seam through all layers, close to the tape edge, and turn through. The loops stand proud of the fabric edge.

BRAID/CORD BUTTON LOOPS

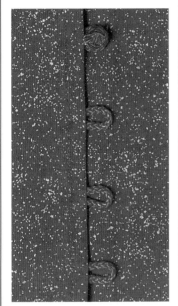

Another quick method, braid or cord loops are formed from a length of cord, looped at intervals. To calculate the length of cord or braid needed, measure the edge to be fastened and double this measurement.

To apply cord loops

1 Make a loop-placement guide from paper, approximately 1½ in (4cm) wide by the length of area to be looped.

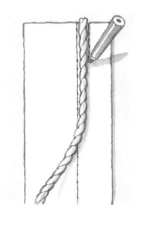

2 Draw a line from top to bottom, ⅝ in (15mm) from one edge. Place braid on the line and mark cord width to the right. Draw a second line the cord width away from first line. ▲

3 Mark loop placements between the parallel lines, spacing them evenly apart.

4 Starting at one end, place cord within parallel lines, forming the first loop. Tape loop in place and then try a button to check it will fit before continuing to form the loops. Baste in place. ▼

5 Fold the paper guide so the straight edge of the taped loops is on the garment edge. Pin and then stitch to right side of garment edge before removing paper guide and basting threads. Continue to assemble garment following pattern instructions. ▲

SELF-FABRIC BUTTON LOOPS

These are made from bias strips of the main garment or project fabric and can be wrapped around the cord or left plain.

1 Cut a length of main fabric on the bias (diagonally from selvage to selvage) approximately ¾ in (20mm) wide by the length needed. If necessary, sew two or more lengths together.

2 Cut a length of string, 5 in (13cm) longer than the bias strip. Lay the string along fabric and fold fabric, right sides together, sandwiching the string.

3 Stitch across top edge through fabric and string, and then down side edge taking ⅜ in (10mm) seam allowance. Avoid catching the string. Do not trim the seam allowances as these will provide filling for the tubing. ▼

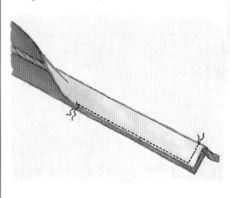

4 Turn through to right side by pulling string through. Cut off the string. ▼

5 Cut fabric tube into loops, large enough to accommodate button and have seam allowances of ⅝ in (15mm) at both ends.

6 Again make a placement guide as steps 1–3 above. Then pin or tape loops to guide with raw edges facing guide edge. ▼

7 Fold placement guide so that the raw edges of the loops are on the garment edge. Pin and stitch loops to garment before removing paper guide.

HAND-STITCHED BUTTON LOOPS

These are ideal for closures that require little strength, for instance at the top of dress openings.

1 Sew button in position. Working with the corresponding garment piece, line up and mark the loop placement.

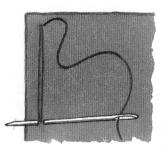

2 Using strong buttonhole thread, secure thread at first placement mark and then take a long stitch to the other placement mark. Leave enough thread in the stitch to form the loop (try the button for size). Stitch two or three long stitches like this. ▲

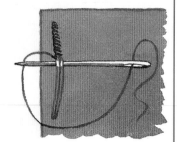

3 Use a closely stitched blanket stitch to form the bottonhole loop. ▲

BOUND BUTTONHOLES

These are another designer touch to finish a garment and may be used on jackets or coats. They are stitched in the same manner as welt pockets (see Welt pockets, page 65). ▲

TIP *Frogs are often used on Chinese-style clothing or where the closure doesn't have to take much strain.*

FROGS AND TOGGLES

These are the names given to decorative fastenings. Toggles are generally used to add a sporty touch, while frogs have a more decorative feel. Hand stitch in place using buttonhole thread. ▼

HOOKS AND EYES

These metal closures can be used alone or at the top of other fasteners such as zippers. They range in size and weight and are available in black or silver. The eye section can be looped or a straight edge. Sew the hook on the overlap and the eye on the underlap. Sew by hand, using either double thread or heavier-weight buttonhole thread. ▼

SNAPS

Snaps are another alternative when the closure will not need to take too much strain and are ideal on young children's clothing or bed linen as they are easy to do up. Decorative snaps are used in place of buttons on loose-fitting garments. ▼

Snaps, like hook and eyes, come in two parts, a socket and a ball. Place the ball section on the underlap or inside of the item. Place the socket section on the overlap or outside of the item. To prevent stitches showing on the right side of a garment, pick up just one or two fibers from the main fabric and, between stitches, tunnel the thread between the layers. Stitch two or three times in each hole.

SNAP TAPE

Small, plastic snaps are available on tapes, with snaps evenly spaced apart. These are ideal both for babywear and for quilt covers. The tape can be machine stitched into position by stitching along both long edges.

1 Separate tape sections. Pin and stitch the ball section to garment or bed linen edge, stitching along both long edges. Work both in the same direction.

2 Pin the socket section to the corresponding edge, matching snaps. ▼

3 Machine stitch as before.

HOOK-AND-LOOP FASTENERS

Another two-part fastener, one side has soft loops and the other stiff hooks. There is now a version with both soft loops and hooks on one tape, which is self-sealing. Hook-and-loop fasteners can be stitched, or stuck to hard surfaces with fusible backing. ▲

SELF-COVERED BUTTONS

If matching buttons are impossible to find, try using self-cover buttons. These are available in white plastic or silver metal in a variety of different sizes. ▼

Instructions to cover the buttons are included in the pack. However, the following tips will help provide a professional finish:

• If using fine fabrics, first cover metal buttons with lightweight woven interfacing. Use a double layer.

• Avoid loosely woven or very bulky fabrics as they will be difficult to gather and clip behind the button—instead use a similar colored alternative fabric.

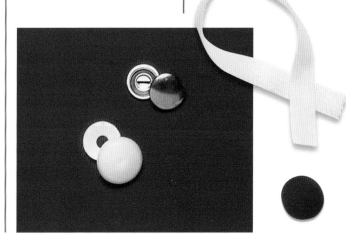

Hemming

There are a variety of hemming techniques used to hem garments, curtains, blinds, and voiles. Which technique to use depends on the type of fabric being sewn and the use of the item.

HEMMING TIPS

• If possible leave hemming until the garment or curtains have hung for at least 24 hours so the fabric can drop and settle. This may result in an uneven hem edge, which can therefore be straightened prior to finishing. This is particularly important for knit fabrics, garments with a bias cut, or loosely woven fabrics.

• The hem can be used to add weight to the lower edge, helping the garment or curtain to hang properly. A good hem depth for straight dresses, skirts, and coats, is 2–3 in (5–7.5cm).

For A-line or flared hems, make a smaller hem of 1¼–2 in (3–5cm), while a good hem allowance for pants is 1¼ in (3cm). Curtains can have hems ranging from 2–6 in (5–15cm).

• To determine an accurate hem length, measure up from the floor to desired hem length, rather than from the waist down. Wear shoes that will be worn with the garment to ensure the back and front will be even. Mark the hemline with chalk or pins placed horizontally, working along the curtain or around the garment. ▼

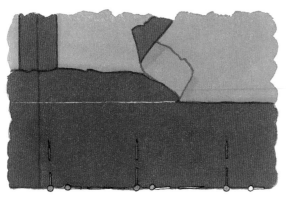

GENERAL HEMMING TECHNIQUES

1 Working from the wrong side, turn the hem allowance up at the marked hemline, matching side seams, and inserting pins at right angles close to the folded edge. Trim the hem allowance to the depth required so that it is even all around. ▲ ▼

2 Ease stitch ¼ in (6mm) from the raw edge of hem allowance with a slightly loosened tension.

3 Working on a flat surface, gently pull up the bobbin thread to take up excess at curves, etc. Spread excess evenly and pin in place.

TAPED HEMS

Finishing a hem with tape or lace edging provides a very neat finish to the inside of a garment as well as possibly extending the hem allowance (by the depth of the tape)—ideal when lengthening garments or lowering the hems of drapes. Bias binding, ribbon, braid or lace edging are all good options. Satin tape is less bulky than cotton tape and stretch lace is ideal for lightweight fabrics.

1 The amount of tape needed is the circumference of the hem, plus 2–5 in (5–13cm) for curves, corners, or turnings.

2 Measure hem length as in the Hemming tips above.

3 Next, working on the right side of fabric, pin, then machine one long edge of tape ¼ in (6mm) from raw edge of fabric, as shown above right. (If using bias binding, pin tape, still folded, with folded side to right side of the garment fabric.)

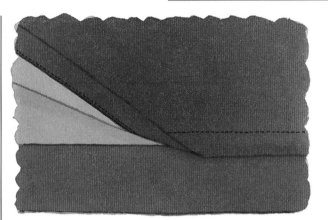

4 Fold hem up at hemline and blind stitch in place. (For blind hemming instructions, see Common stitches and sewing terms, page 34.) ▼

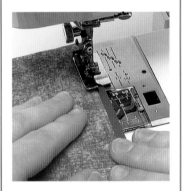

Hemming leathers and suedes

Leather and suedes are treated differently because it is not always desirable to see stitches on the right side (when top stitching) nor is it possible to blind hem by hand (as there are no fibers to pick up). However, leather and suede can be hemmed by using fusible-hemming webs.

Alternatively, on heavyweight leather, simply cut the hem level at the hemline.

1 To apply fusible webbing, first turn hem allowance up at hemline. If necessary, pound in place with a tailor's block.

2 Trim hem allowance to between ⅝–2 in (15mm–5cm), depending on the garment.

3 Place the webbing under the hem allowance and press in place, using a press cloth and medium hot dry iron. (Do not use steam, which may shrink or color the leather.) ▲

Hemming linings

Linings are most often hemmed with a double-machine-stitched hem. Sometimes the hems of lining and main garment are hemmed separately, at other times they are hemmed together and "bagged out." Jackets may have lining and main fabric hemmed together—this means the lining and main garment are stitched, right sides together, all around, leaving a turning gap through which the garment is turned before slip stitching the gap closed. Skirts, dresses, and curtains usually have linings that hang separately. The lining hem should be shorter than the main garment hem so that it sits just above the garment or curtain hem. The ideal length is so that it comes just over the top of the garment hem fold.

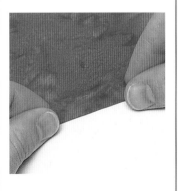

1 Fold the hem allowance to wrong side at hemline. ▲

2 Trim hem allowance to ¾ in (2cm) and then turn under raw edge to meet first fold. ▲ ▼

3 Machine stitch in place and then press.

TIP *Always pre-wash fabric and lining to prevent uneven shrinkage at later laundering.*

SEWING WITH SPECIAL FABRICS

Some fabrics require special care and attention. For instance, sheers need neat seams that look good on the inside and out, bulky fabrics and faux furs need special trimming techniques, while beaded fabrics need careful handling.

SHEERS AND LACES

These include chiffon, georgette, voile, organdy, dotted swiss, and organza, as well as cluny lace, chantilly lace, and all-over lacy fabrics. Typical uses are blouses, dresses, tops, and over-tops.

Machine needles 9–11 (60–75) sharps or universal
Stitch length per inch 12–15 (1.8–2mm)
Seam type French seams, double stitched or rolled.

Sewing sheers and laces

1 Hold fabric taut at front and back when stitching. If seams still pucker when being stitched, add a layer of tissue to the seam line. Once stitched, tear away the tissue.

2 Eliminate the hem allowance on scalloped-edge laces. For laces, cut hem allowance to a bare minimum ⅜–⅝ in (10–15mm), turn up and hand stitch. For sheers, make a rolled hem by hand or machine. Alternatively, bind the hem edge with a fine satin bias tape or lace edging.

TIP *Use a small-hole throat plate on the sewing machine to prevent the fabric being pulled down into the feed dogs.*

Lace

Sometimes it is desirable to match the lace design at seams, for instance, on center front or back seams so that it looks like one continuous piece.

1 Place the paper pattern over a single layer of lace so the seam line runs through the center of the motifs. Mark the seam line with chalk or basting thread.

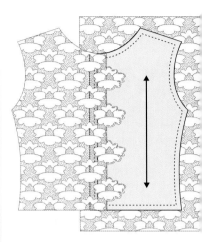

2 Thread trace around the lace design, outside seam line. ▲

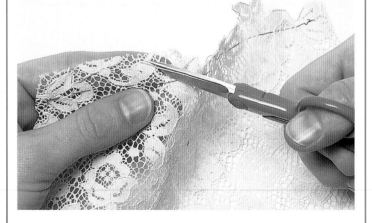

3 Cut around traced design. ▲

4 Lay the corresponding pattern piece over the cut-out section, matching seam lines. Trace the overlapping motif onto the pattern tissue.

5 Pin the marked tissue to a single layer of lace, matching overlapped design and seam lines. Again thread trace the seam line. Cut out pattern piece.

6 Lap the lace sections, matching the seam line. Again trace thread around the motif as for step 2 above, then machine stitch through both layers. ▲

7 Using small sharp scissors, trim away the overlapping edges. Press carefully to avoid crushing the lace. ▲

BEADED/SEQUIN FABRICS

These beautifully decorated fabrics are best used on very simple garments with minimum seaming and few pieces. Typical uses are eveningwear, dresses, or tops.

Machine needles 9–11 (60–75) depending on the base fabric
Stitch length per inch 10–15 (1.8–2.5mm)
Seam type Straight seams.

Beads need to be trimmed from the seam allowance to prevent bulk or awkward ripples and bulges. However, as the sequins or beads are often stitched to the fabric with one continuous thread, it is not possible to simply cut them off. Instead:

• Crush beads individually (use a little hammer or two spoons) and then pick off the bits.

• Carefully snip away sequins without cutting the thread.

Sewing beaded or sequin fabrics

1 Cut out in single layers, turning pattern pieces over to get right and left sides if necessary. Use the "with nap" layout.

2 Press on a soft surface such as a folded towel to prevent crushing the beads and always press on the reverse with a press cloth. Avoid steam or moisture, which may damage the beads and discolor the sequins.

3 Cut facings from lining fabric rather than a layer of the beaded fabric. Use sew-in interfacings rather than fusibles.

4 Use a zipper foot to sew seams if the beads prevent straight stitching.

TIP *Use old scissors when cutting heavily beaded fabric as beads and sequins can blunt shears quickly.*

PILE AND "WITH NAP" FABRICS

These include fleece, faux fur, suede, leather, brushed cotton, and brushed denim. Because of the wide range of fabrics in this category, they can be used for a huge variety of garments from luxury eveningwear to soft furnishings.

Machine needles 12–16 (80–100) Leather wedge point for leather; jeans needles for denim and faux fur; ball point needles for pile fabrics such as stretch velour and fleece.

Stitch length per inch 5–8 (3.5–6 mm)

Seam type Plain, straight seam on fur, fleece, brushed fabrics. Lapped or welt on leather and suede.

Sewing with pile or "with nap" fabrics

1 Cut pieces on a single layer of fabric, flipping pattern over to get left and right sides. Stitch in the direction of the pile or nap.

TIP *When pressing pile fabrics, use a needleboard, soft terry towel or layer of self fabric. Always press from the reverse using a press cloth. Avoid steam on leather and suede fabrics.*

2 Trim fur pile from seam allowance to reduce bulk. ▲

3 Use a pin to pick out pile trapped in seam stitching. ▼

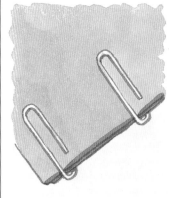

TIP *Follow the "with nap" layout on all fabrics with pile or surface detail. Use paper clips or basting tape rather than pins to hold the leather and suede sections together.*

VELVET

There are a number of types of velvet, which can be made from cotton, silk, or a mixture of man-made fibers for added stretch. Velvets include devoré (in which areas of velvet pile are burned away to create a pattern), velveteen (a lighter-weight, short-pile fabric), panné (a soft, short-pile fabric with pile flattened in one direction) and crushed velvet (which has a crushed pile). Velvet is usually used for luxury eveningwear, jackets, wraps, dresses, and pants.

Machine needles 9–11 (60–75) sharps or ballpoint for stretch velvets

Stitch length per inch 10–12 (2–2.5mm)

Seam type Plain or zigzag stitch for stretch velvets.

TIP *As velvets can "walk" when sewn, which causes the layers to feed through the machine unevenly, always use an even-feed foot or walking foot to keep layers together. Also pin closely together.*

STRETCH FABRICS

These include single knits, jerseys, T-shirt knits, double knits, and swimwear fabrics such as Lycra™. Knits are most commonly used for sportswear, casual wear, and of course, swimwear. Single knits are also ideal for tops, dresses, and comfort-fit lingerie.

Knit fabrics can be cut slightly smaller than actual size if a close fit is desired. Seam edges on knits do not need neatening. However, to prevent them curling, stitch a double row and trim close to the stitching. If using a straight stitch, stretch as you go to provide some flexibility. ▼

Sewing with velvet

1 Cut out pieces from a single layer of fabric, flipping pattern to get a right and left side.

2 Finish seams with zigzag stitch or by binding. Stitch in the direction of the nap. ▲

3 Use a needleboard or self fabric as pressing board. Press from reverse using a press cloth.

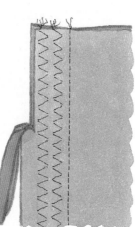

Stabilize areas that are not supposed to stretch (for example, shoulder seams, or V-necklines) by using stay stitch or edge tape fused to the wrong side. Use woven or stretch interfacings. ▼

TIP *When adding elastic to swimwear, choose lingerie elastic or clear elastic that is resistant to perspiration.*

Hemming stretch fabrics

Hem with blind hem stitch or double top stitch. Other good hem techniques are lettuce edging and shell-tucked hems, both of which work well on stretch fabrics. ▼

Machine needles Ball point needles, 9–11 (60–75) for single knits; 11–14 (75–90) for double knits and swimwear.
Stitch length per inch 12–15 (1.8–2mm) for single knits; 10–12 (2–2.5mm) for double knits and swimwear.
Seam type Stretch stitch or zigzag stitch so that the seam still has flexibility.

STRIPES AND PLAIDS

All types of fabric can be striped, checked, or have a plaid design, but whatever fabric composition, they need to be handled carefully in order to match stripes and checks.

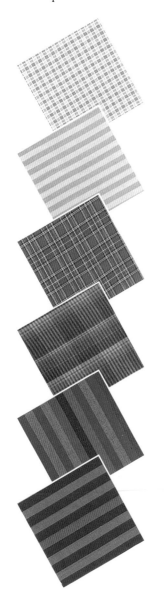

Plaids have lengthwise and crosswise stripes or bars, which can be even or uneven in design. All plaids also have a dominant stripe, both vertically and horizontally. Checks and stripes can also be even or uneven in design. Stripes have either horizontal or vertical lines to follow and are therefore easier to match.

Machine needles and stitch length Depending on fabric weight and type.
Seam type Plain, lapped, or stretch, depending on the fabric type.

Matching plaids

• Only use stripes and plaids with commercial patterns if they are listed among the "suggested fabrics." They are only listed when it has been checked that they work.

• Choose patterns with a minimal number of pieces.

• Use the "with nap" layout.

• Cut from a single layer of fabric, placing tissue pieces carefully so the dominant stripes are not placed at widest points, that is, chest, hips, or hemline. Flip pattern to cut right and left sides, matching checks/stripes at same point on pattern pieces. Remember to

 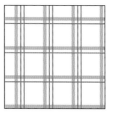

| Stripe | Plaid | Check |

discount seam allowances when matching design. The stripes or checks will not match at all seams, so pick the most prominent places for pattern matching.

• To match plaids and checks will require more fabric than a plain or all-over pattern fabric.

TIP To determine the most dominant stripe in a plaid, hang a fabric length on a door and step back a few paces. The most prominent stripe will stand out.

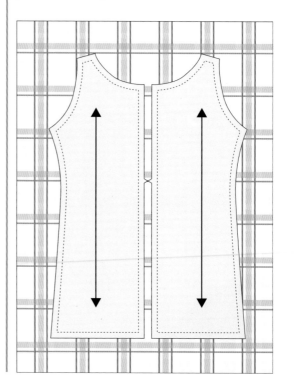

CREATIVE SEWING

There are many ways to sew creatively, often using the simplest of stitches. Master simple techniques such as patchwork and quilting; stumpwork and trapunto; raw-edge, reverse, shadow, and mola appliqués. You can also use your sewing as paint and the fabric as canvas to create textural art with free-motion machine embroidery.

PATCHWORK AND QUILTING

Patchwork is the term used to sew blocks of fabric together while quilting is the term for sewing layers together, with batting sandwiched between the layers. Patchwork and quilting are usually combined—fabrics are pieced together, layered with the backing and batting and then quilted together.

Terminology

Backing The layer of fabric that backs the quilt. Although traditionally muslin, it can be any fabric that complements the quilt.

Sashing   Border   Binding

Squares   Block   Backing

Batting Also known as wadding, this is the non-woven filler material sandwiched between the quilt and the backing. The thickness or loft chosen creates the desired amount of puffiness or dimensional thickness around the quilting stitches (loft refers to the thickness and weight of batting).

Blocks The term used to describe the pieced sets of fabric making up the pattern repeated across the quilt.

Border The strips of fabrics added around the quilted section that border the piece.

Chain piecing This is a time-saving technique for joining a series of pieces together. A short length of thread is left in-between the joined pairs, which is cut apart once the chain is finished. Also known as assembly-line piecing.

Fat quarters Many patchwork and quilting cottons are sold in fat quarters that are ¼ yard (meter) squares of fabric. Often sold in color co-ordinated groups or prints.

Scrap quilt A quilt made up of fabric scraps left over from other sewing projects. They are made from a variety of different fabric types, scrap quilts often have a unique "unplanned" look and are also known as crazy patchwork.

FABRICS

Fabrics need to be light to medium weight and colorfast. The best fabric is 100% cotton, which is easily laundered and sewn. Ideally, fabrics should be washed and pressed prior to use, to allow for shrinkage and fading. If colors do run, soak in a solution of three parts water to one part vinegar.

Templates

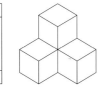
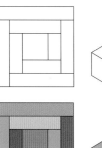

Log cabin *Tumbling blocks* *Flying geese* *Ohio star*

There are many traditional types of patchwork designs, including the popular Log cabin, Flying geese, Ohio star, Tumbling blocks, and Baby blocks.

Most patchwork combinations require pieces to be very accurately cut, and thus use of templates is advisable. These can be cut from either cardboard or plastic and should always include seam allowances (usually ¼ in [6mm]).

Simple squares, triangles, and rectangles can be cut quickly and in multiples using a rotary cutter, self-healing grid mat, and ruler (preferably see-through).

Before starting, make sure the fabric edge is straight by folding the fabric in half, with selvages together. With ruler at right angles to the fold, cut a straight edge.

Rotate opened fabric so cut edge is along edge of cutting mat. Measure width of strip to be cut (remember to add seam allowances to both sides), mark at various points along the length to ensure accuracy. Hold ruler in place and cut the strips. Several layers can be cut at once, providing the layers are anchored together well. To do this, either hand baste or pin regularly throughout the layers. ▼

Piecing
Piecing of the cut fabric can be done by hand or machine.

By hand Mark the stitching line ¼ in (6mm) from edge and join two pieces, right sides together. Hand stitch along one edge only, beginning and ending at the stitching line, not the fabric edge. Continue in this manner, piecing pairs until you are ready to sew blocks together. Then sew the blocks into strips and finally the strips together.

By machine Adjust the needle position to give a ¼ in (6mm) seam or use a special ¼ in (6mm) quilting foot. Pair patches, right sides together, and stitch along one edge. Alternatively, chain piece several pairs together at the same time (see Terminology, page 125, for an explanation of chain piecing). ▼

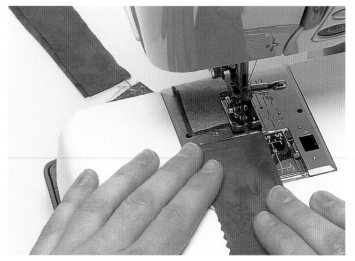

Border

Butted corner

Mitered corner

This frames the finished quilt top. It can have butted or mitered corners with strips joined at 90-degree angles. The simplest method is the butted border. ▲

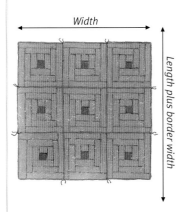

Width

Length plus border width

1 To determine the fabric required for the border, measure the width and cut two lengths (for top and bottom). Next measure the length, adding the top/bottom border width. Cut two pieces (for side edges). ▲

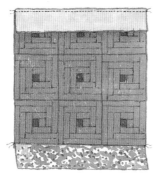

2 Machine stitch top and bottom borders to quilt, right sides together, again taking a ¼ in (6mm) seam allowance. ▲

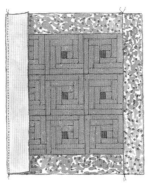

3 Next add side borders, which should go the entire length from top to bottom of the border at the foot of the quilt. ▲

PREPARING TO QUILT

Once the fabric pieces are all together in the chosen design the work can be quilted. If there is to be a specific quilt design, it should be marked onto the quilt top before the quilt is sandwiched.

Alternative quilting methods are to stitch "in the ditch" (stitch along the seam lines of the joined pieces, working from the right side), use a range of quilting stitches such as stippling stitch (see below), or by free-motion stitching (with feed dogs down).

TIP *If marking a quilting design on the fabric, use a method that is easily erased. Always test on a scrap of quilting fabric first and do not iron marked areas as the marks may be set into the fabric by the heat.*

The quilt sandwich

1 Prepare the batting by opening it out and letting the creases drop out. Cut batting at least 2 in (5cm) larger than the total quilt size as the process of quilt stitching will make it shrink in size.

2 Cut the backing fabric, approximately 3 in (8cm) larger than the quilt top to allow for shrinkage when quilting.

3 Press the quilt top (if not marked with a marking pen) and backing fabric before sandwiching the batting between the layers. Lay backing fabric right side down on a flat surface. Add batting and then quilt on top, right side uppermost, matching centers of all layers and pinning through. ▲

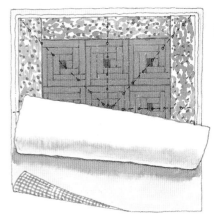

4 Baste the layers together with quilting pins, basting spray, or hand-basting stitches in a contrast color. Work from the center out to the sides for each line of basting. ▲

QUILTING

Quilt stitching can be done by hand or machine. Machining is obviously much quicker but it can take practice. A number of designs can be used, including straight, zigzag, satin, blanket, herringbone, or stippling stitches.

By hand Use a "betweens" needle, which is short and sharp, and sewing thread that is slightly heavier than normal (or decorative thread). If possible, use a frame to support the area of quilt being stitched (but do not leave the quilt in frame overnight as it may leave permanent creases).

TIP *Run hand-stitching thread through a wax block to prevent tangles.*

1 Cut a thread length approximately 18 in (46cm). Knot one end.

2 Start quilting from the center, working out to the side edges. Make first stitch from back to front, tugging on thread slightly to pull the knot into batting. Make 3–4 back stitches before starting a row.

3 Make short rows of stitches, taking care to keep each stitch the same length.

4 Use your free hand to guide the needle at the back of work. Finish with a backstitch or two.

By machine This can be done using normal stitching techniques or free motion. Again, start at the center of the quilt and work outward.

Normal stitching

1 Use a walking foot or even-feed foot, which helps the layers of fabric pass through the machine without shifting or puckering (some machines have a differential feed motion for quilting—check your user manual). ▼

2 Test stitch on a sample of the quilting, batting, and backing to check tension, stitch length, etc.

3 Choose your stitch design. For instance, stitch in the ditch works well on straight-edged patterns, stitching on the flattest side of the seam (the one without seam

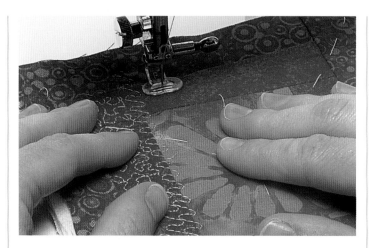

allowances underneath), using matching or invisible thread.

4 For repeated straight lines use a quilting bar, which is L-shaped and usually found in the sewing-machine accessories box. It fixes onto the presser foot and the spacing can be adjusted from ½–4 in (13mm–10cm).

5 Stippling stitch is a particular machine stitch that produces a random looking coverage of curvaceous stitching. To stipple,

you need a stippling foot or darning foot. Drop the feed dogs and move the fabric slowly as the stitches form. Some embroidery and quilting machines have a built-in stippling stitch. ▲

Free-motion quilting

The benefit of this technique is that the quilt can be moved up, down, right, left, diagonally, etc., without turning it. The length of stitch is determined by how much the quilt is moved.

1 Lower the feed dogs—there is normally a dial or button under the accessory case (see your user manual for directions) or tape over the feed dogs.

2 Use a darning foot and reduce the stitch length to 0.

3 Lower the presser foot (to engage the tension) and start stitching, moving the quilt so as to change direction and stitch length.

Trapunto

Trapunto is a quilting technique that produces a raised surface pattern. It originated in Italy in the early 16th century and traditional designs included vines, leaves, grapes, cherries, etc. The outline of the design is stitched with a straight stitch through a top and backing fabric. The raised texture is then created by stuffing between the backing and top fabric. Traditonally, vines and straight-line patterns were threaded with a soft yarn or cording, while the rounded shapes were stuffed with batting inserted into a small slit made in the backing fabric, which was then slip stitched. Nowadays there are three main ways to create trapunto.

ADDING A LAYER OF BATTING

This is sandwiched between the top and backing fabric so that the design areas stitched will be held firmly together but the spaces and open areas between the stitching will puff up. The alternative way to use the batting technique is to heavily stitch the design, which will then lie flat against a puffed background.

Steps to sew

1 Draw the design outline on the right side of the top fabric using a vanishing marking pen or chalk pencil.

TIP *Before stitching the project, check the stitch length and tension by testing combinations on a sample comprising the same type and number of layers.*

2 Sandwich a layer of batting between the top fabric and backing fabric (muslin or medium-weight cotton) so the wrong sides of top and backing fabric are next to the batting. ▲

3 Using a straight stitch, stitch the design outline. (For small design areas, consider filling the area with stitching so the padding outlines the design).

4 If desired, carefully cut away excess batting around the design so that only the design area is padded. ▲

CORDING

Again a top and backing fabric are used together. The design is stitched out, using two parallel rows and then, working from the back, cord or yarn is fed between the rows of stitching.

Steps to sew

1 Draw the design outline, following the batting technique. Pin top and backing fabrics, wrong sides together.

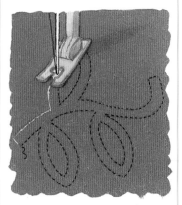

2 Stitch two parallel rows of stitching for the design outline (or use a twin needle). ▲

3 Carefully make a small slit in the backing fabric only, and thread cord or yarn between the parallel rows using a blunt-tipped needle (darning needle). ▲ ▼

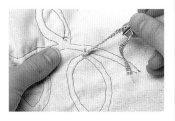

4 For larger, rounded areas of the design, slit the backing and stuff with batting before slip stitching the slit closed. ▼

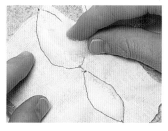

Using a trapunto gun

This shoots fluffy yarn between top and backing fabrics to fill unstitched spaces (the design is stitched with straight stitch). The gun uses compressed air to blow yarn from its cone through a needle.

STUMPWORK

Stumpwork is an intricate dimensional embroidery, raised and padded with design elements in high relief. It can be dated back to the 17th century when designs invariably consisted of doll-like figures in a garden full of flowers and animals. Stumpwork was found on boxes, cabinets, small bags, and mirrors. Stumpwork employs a wide range of embroidery techniques including stitches such as chain, whipped, stem, and buttonhole stitch, French knots, couching techniques, and appliqué.

Steps to sew

1 Trace or draw your design onto the right side of the main fabric.

2 Add a layer of backing fabric (muslin is ideal) and place both in an embroidery hoop.

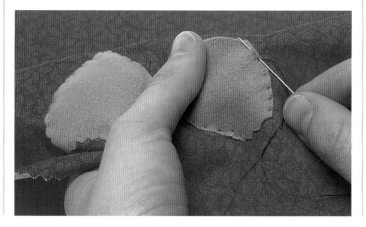

3 Embroider the design using chosen stitches, for instance stem stitch to fill in the leaves, and chain stitch for outline areas. ▼

4 Add appliqué pieces by prick stitching (making tiny running stitches on the right side) in place or by machine stitching using blanket stitch, layering them or padding them with a little stuffing. ▼

5 Embroider other elements on a separate hoop, by stitching over wire, etc. and then applying them to the main work. Add buttons, etc. for a three-dimensional finish.

Chenille

Traditional chenille is a textural fabric finish that looks soft and fluffy. It can be reproduced by stitching together several layers of fabric and then cutting through the upper layers (leaving just the base layer intact). Once laundered and dried, the cut edges fray and provide the soft fluffy appearance of chenille. Chenille fabric can be used for cushion covers, to make bags, as panels in bedspreads, or as decorative detailing on garments.

The best fabrics to use are those that fray easily such as 100% cotton, denim, challis, tweed, and coarse-weave fabrics. Choice of colors is also important as each layer can be glimpsed in the chenille cut. The top layer will be the main color, the next layer will provide visual texture, and the third layer should be a good contrast with the base layer. Appliqué can also be included on the top layer for added pattern.

Steps to sew

1 Cut the base layer so that it is at least 1 in (25mm) larger all around than the other layers.

2 Add three or more layers of fabric, all right side uppermost. (Fuse appliqué in place to top fabric before layering.) Pin all layers together.

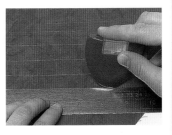

3 Mark a 45-degree line across the top layer then mark parallel lines either side of this first line, each approximately ½ in (13mm) apart. ▲

> **TIP** If the fabric layers fail to feed evenly, then use a walking foot.

4 Straight stitch along the lines, starting and finishing at the overlapping base layer. ▼

5 Using a pair of long sharp scissors or a slash cutter, cut all but the base layer through the channels created by the rows of stitching. (A slash cutter is a rotary cutter with an additional base strip, which prevents cutting the bottom layer.) ▲

> **TIP** If you do accidentally cut through the base layer, simply add a patch to the underside. Stitch this in place along the previous stitching lines.

6 Wash and dry the chenille piece and then finish as a cushion cover, table runner, or a panel in a garment.

Appliqué

Alternative appliqués can be applied to add creative embellishments and decorations to sewn fabrics. We start with raw-edge appliqué—an easy technique to master and a great beginner's choice—and move on to more complex shadow and mola appliqués.

RAW-EDGE APPLIQUÉ

The idea of this type of appliqué is that the edges do fray a little to give it a "raw" feel. Although the edges are to be frayed, they need to be even and thus a simple geometric or square design is preferable. Fabrics to use include cottons, hessian, calico, etc. An alternative to leaving them completely raw is to pink the edges with pinking shears.

1 Cut out the design to be appliquéd from appliqué fabric. Remember to add ½ in (13mm) of seam allowance.

2 Using a straight stitch, machine around the appliqué, ½ in (13mm) from the outer edge.

3 Apply double-sided fusible web within the stitching of the appliqué panel. Fuse appliqué to the main fabric.

4 Again using a straight stitch, or a decorative stitch, machine stitch motif to main fabric, working approximately ⅛ in (3mm) from previous stitching lines, keeping the outer edge of the appliqué free.

5 Draw threads from the edges of the appliqué until a pleasing result is achieved. ▼

REVERSE APPLIQUÉ

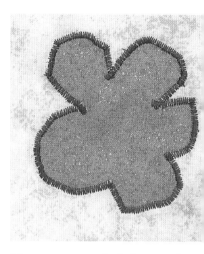

There are two methods for reverse appliqué. The first is a simple method to use when working with intricate designs, and the second produces a 3-D effect.

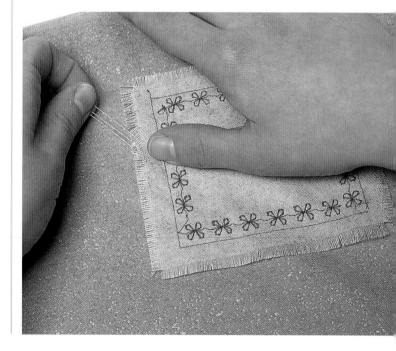

Simple reverse method

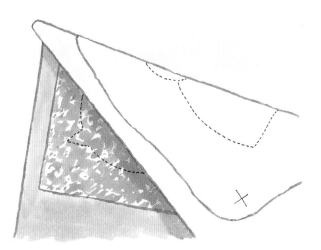

1 Interface the main fabric and draw design on interfacing. ▲

2 Pin the wrong side of a large piece of appliqué fabric to the right side of the fabric within the guidelines.

3 Working from the back, straight stitch around the design.

4 Turn work to right side and cut out carefully around the design, cutting close to the stitching. ▼

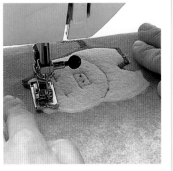

5 Finish with satin or zigzag stitch to cover raw edges. ▲

3-D effect

1 Fuse interfacing to the back of the main fabric where the appliqué will be placed.

2 Mark guide lines for the design area on the interfacing and then place a piece of appliqué fabric within the guide lines, right side to interfacing.

TIP *For the appliqué, choose a fabric that doesn't unravel too easily, such as cotton, fleece, or gabardine.*

3 Draw the design on the reverse of the appliqué fabric. ▲

TIP *Use either water-soluble or fadeaway marker pens when transferring the design to the interfacing.*

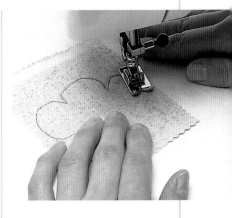

4 Using a straight stitch, and working from the back, stitch the outline of the design. ▲

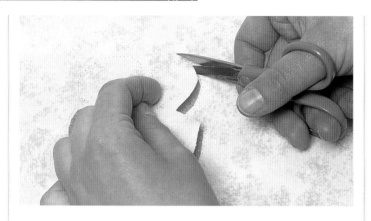

5 Working from right side, cut away main fabric and interfacing within the straight stitched lines. Cut close to stitching. ▲

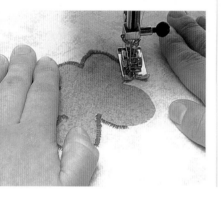

6 Finish with a satin stitch or narrow zigzag stitch around the cut edges to cover the raw edges. If required, trim away excess appliqué fabric from the back of the work. ◄ ▼

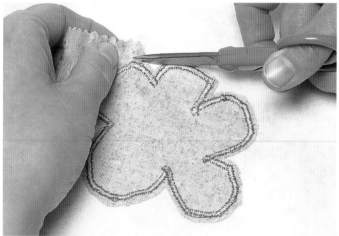

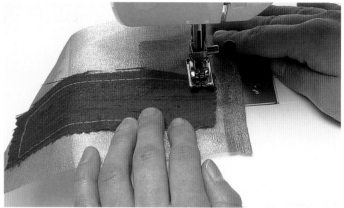

SHADOW APPLIQUÉ

Stitched in the same manner as 3-D reverse appliqué, shadow appliqué works well on lightweight and almost transparent fabrics, as the appliqué shows through from the back.

1 Draw design onto right side of main fabric using a chalk pencil or fadeaway marking pen.

2 Machine baste a piece of appliqué fabric in position under the main fabric. ▲

3 Select an appliqué stitch, such as satin stitch or narrow zigzag stitch, and stitch the design, working from the right side.

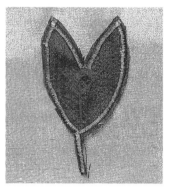

4 Turn work to the reverse and cut away excess appliqué fabric from around the design. ▲ ▼

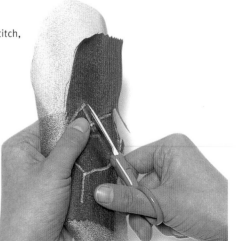

MOLA APPLIQUÉ

Molas originate from the San Blas region of Panama and were made in bright colors by the Kuna Indians. Molas often combine the different appliqué methods of traditional straight appliqué (see Finishing touches, page 104), reverse, and inlay. The fabrics most commonly used are tightly woven cotton fabrics. These appliqués can be added to many projects, such as pillow covers, bags, jacket fronts or backs.

Mola reverse

The reverse appliqué method for a mola appliqué is similar to the reverse method above. However, many different-colored fabrics are layered together and the upper layers are cut to different thicknesses to show the vibrant colors beneath. The layers are then stitched around the cut-out shapes to hold them together.

1 Layer three or four different colored fabrics, all with right side uppermost. Machine baste together around the edges. ▼

2 Trace a design to be cut out onto the top layer using a chalk pencil or vanishing marking pen. Use easy shapes such as geometric shapes.

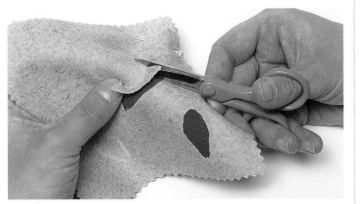

3 Carefully cut one of the design areas from the top layer only. ▲

4 Turn under the raw edges a scant ⅛ in (3mm) around the cut edge.

5 Hand stitch with tiny running stitches or machine stitch with a decorative stitch to hold the layers together.

6 Repeat for another design on the top layer, this time cutting through more layers. ▲

TIP *Hold the top layer away from other layers with a pin as you snip into it for the first cut.*

Mola inlay

Very similar to the reverse method, the inlay fabrics are small pieces sandwiched between the base and top fabric. These then appear as "windows" when the top layer is cut through. This method has the advantage of being less bulky than the reverse method as there are only three layers of fabric involved.

1 Trace a design on the right side of the top fabric, again using simple geometric shapes.

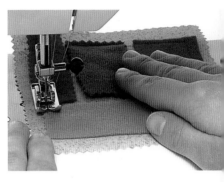

2 Sandwich small colored fabric pieces between the base and top fabric, all with right sides uppermost, positioning the small pieces where the design will be cut out. ▲▼

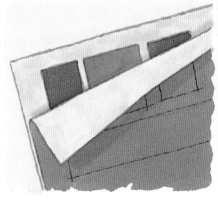

3 Cut out one design area, turn under raw edges and stitch in place as before, working each design area completely before moving onto another.

Free-motion embroidery

Free-motion embroidery is a creative alternative to machine-stitching embroideries that come on special disks or as part of the stitch library on today's computerized embroidery machines. It is the term used to describe stitching in any direction, with stitches of any length.

THE BASICS

Sewing machine
There is no need for a top-of-the-line machine—one that can straight stitch and zigzag stitch is all that is required.

Feed dogs To free-motion embroider it is necessary to lower the feed dogs. These are the serrated caterpillar tracks that come up through the throat plate under the presser foot. Normally they move backward and forward and help feed the fabric through when stitching. When they are lowered they no longer move the fabric and thus it can be moved at will in any direction.

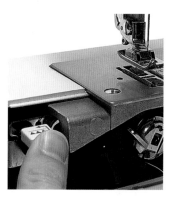

The feed dogs are usually found under the accessory table and can be lowered by lever, disk, or dial.

> **TIP** *If using an older-style machine that doesn't have the ability to lower feed dogs, cover them with thin card taped in position and/or reduce stitch length to 0.*

Pressure on presser foot On many machines the presser-foot lever has to be lowered in order to engage the tension on the top thread. However, for free-motion embroidery, the pressure on the presser foot needs to be released so that it does not hold the fabric.

Darning or stippling foot A darning or stippling foot has a large hole through which the needle can swing wide zigzags, etc. It is also usually made of clear plastic so that you can see the stitching below. It is possible to stitch without a presser foot at all (However, it may still be necessary to lower the lever—try it and see.)

Embroidery hoop A hoop is used to hold the fabric taut as it is stitched. Wooden embroidery hoops or spring hoops are available from most needlework shops. A spring hoop is ideal as it can be tightened to grip the fabric and makes it easier to re-position the fabric. If using a wooden hoop, wrap it in cotton strips, which will help grip the main fabric.

> **TIP** *It is possible to work without a hoop—simply add one or two layers of writing paper under the work to provide stability. These are then ripped off when the stitching is complete.*

Stabilizers These are used to prevent the main fabric from puckering and distorting as it is stitched. Added underneath, they can be tear-away or soluble so that once the stitching is complete, they can be removed (see Stabilizers, page 91 for more details).

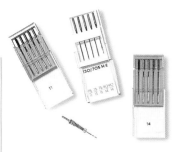

Needles Use embroidery machine needles, of a size determined by the thread and fabric being stitched. For most threads a 10/12 (80/90) size is ideal, while for metallic threads choose a 12/14 (70/80) size needle. Machine-embroidery needles often have a larger than normal eye to cope with the intricate threads. Metallic threads can also cut a small groove in the eye, invisible to the naked eye, and thus should not be re-used for any other type of thread, which may then snag or break on the groove.

Threads Machine-embroidery threads are available in a huge variety of colors and strengths. Most popular is rayon 40, which is a high-luster thread.

Machine-embroidery thread is finer than regular sewing thread because embroidery tends to involve a greater number of closely stitched areas, which requires a large volume of thread. Alternative specialist threads include variegated colors and metallics in different strengths.

When machine embroidering it is advisable to use bobbin fill in the bobbin. This is a lightweight thread, usually in white or black, which again will cut down the amount of thread to be used in densely stitched areas. For free-motion embroidery, it may be desirable to use an unusual bulky or unevenly spun thread. In this case, wind it by hand onto a bobbin and then work with the right side facing the throat plate. Use regular thread in the needle.

Tension Regular sewing requires the top and bobbin thread tensions to be balanced in order for stitches to be formed perfectly.

Bobbin tension Sewing-machine manufacturers do not recommend altering bobbin tension because it can be difficult to correct for general sewing. However, for free-motion embroidery it can be helpful. To alter bobbin tension usually requires turning a screw on the bobbin case. To restrict the flow of bobbin thread, so that it doesn't show on top, tighten the tension. This is ideal for fine work. If a fleck of the thread is preferred (for texture), loosen the screw so that the bobbin thread comes to surface with top thread.

TIP Keep a second bobbin case for machine embroidery so that one is always correct for general sewing.

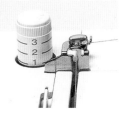

Top tension Again this can be increased or decreased in order to change the texture of the stitches. To increase the amount of bobbin thread showing on the surface, as well as loosening the bobbin screw, tighten the top tension by turning the dial toward either the + or a higher number on the dial. ▲ ▼

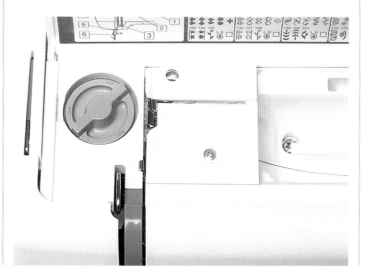

GETTING STARTED

1 Set your machine to stitch width and length 0. Change to a darning or stippling foot and release pressure on the presser foot. If possible, set your machine to stitch slowly.

2 Cut a layer of stabilizer to go behind the main fabric (tear-away or water-soluble stabilizer). ▼

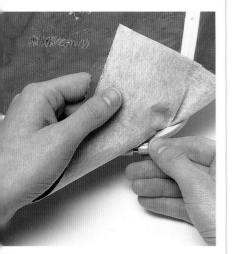

3 Fix work in a hoop by laying the stabilizer then the main fabric, right side up, over the outer ring of the hoop. Press the inner hoop inside the outer, stretching the fabric so it is held taut. Tighten the screw. The hooped work is placed under the needle so the bottom of the fabric and hoop lay flat on the machine bed.

4 Lower the presser foot to engage top tension and then turn the flywheel once to lower and raise the needle, bringing up the bobbin thread.

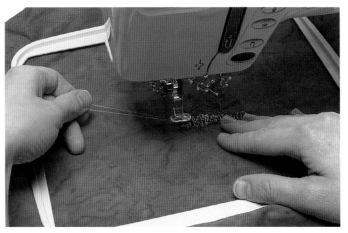

5 Holding both thread tails, take two or three stitches, moving the hoop so the stitching is over the thread tails to secure them. Then cut the remaining tails before continuing. ▲

6 Holding the edges of the hoop, move the work forward for a few stitches, sideways, backward, diagonally, etc. The amount of movement determines the stitch length. ▲

● Use contrasting colors in bobbin and top thread so you can see the effect of altering the tension.

● Use a specialist thread or yarn, hand wound on the bobbin, with regular thread on the top and place work face down in the hoop.

● Couch down specialist yarns to add texture.

EXPERIMENTING WITH DESIGN

Once the basic principles are mastered, try stitching to a design. First mark out the design on the top fabric using a vanishing marker pen or chalk pencil and then, following the steps above, stitch over the design lines using a combination of straight and zigzag stitch.

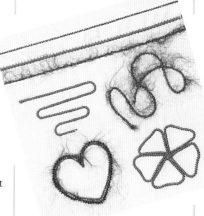

● To fill areas quickly, increase the stitch width to 2 and zigzag stitch forward and backward.

TIP *When stitching, if the fabric starts to pucker or stitches skip, tighten the fabric in the hoop.*

STITCHING LANDSCAPES

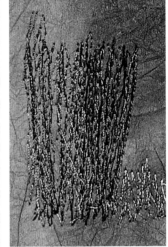

1 Using watered-down fabric paints, colorwash the background to give a general idea of sky, horizon, grass, etc. ▲

2 Once dry, iron the fabric to fix the colors, then stabilize and hoop the work as before.

3 Stitch grasses with long straight stitches, using a variegated green thread. Change to darker and lighter colors to stitch over the grasses again to give depth.

4 Create a sense of scale by using smaller stitches for the distance and large stitches for the foreground.

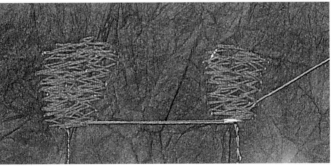

5 Add flowers by stitching in small circles. ▲

6 Use zigzag stitch to fill in areas such as the bark of a tree.

7 To use the same color in different areas, simply move the work to the next position and lower the needle by turning the flywheel. Fix the thread by making two or three stitches over some of the thread trail and then continue. The thread trails can be cut away later by pulling them taut and snipping close to stitching.

8 To create shading, use four or five threads of slightly different shades of the same color. Start with the same shade of top thread and in the bobbin, and work straight stitches in parallel rows. Loosen the tension of the bobbin so that the bobbin thread comes up to the surface. ▲

9 Change the top thread to a lighter or darker shade (shade 2) and work the next few rows.

10 Change the bobbin thread to shade 2, and the top thread to shade 3. Work a few more rows.

11 Change the bobbin thread to shade 3 and the top thread to the shade 4, and so on.

Stabilizers

Stabilizers are used when sewing a densely stitched area—such as buttonholes, appliqué, and machine embroidery—in order to prevent the fabric puckering and distorting. A stabilizer is literally a layer of fabric, usually a non-woven material, which is added to the back and/or front of the work and then removed after stitching. There are a number of types of stabilizer including those that tear away and others that are soluble.

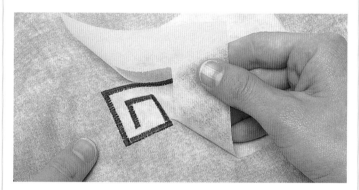

Tear-away stabilizers
• Look like crisp interfacing but have a handle like paper. Available in black or white, use the color tone nearest the color of the fabric.

• Add stabilizer to the back of the work, covering the area that is to be stitched.

• Stitch the design or motif over the stabilizer and then tear the stabilizer from around the stitching. ▲

• If necessary, use a pin or needle to pick out bits from the stitching. Snip into pieces on enclosed areas of stitching and again, tear away.

Self-adhesive embroidery backers
These are used to stabilize small areas on which you wish to add embroidery detail, such as collars, cuffs or hat brims, but which are too small to fill an embroidery frame. The stabilizer is put into the embroidery frame and then an area, slightly larger than the embroidery design is scored with a pin so that the backing can be removed. The fabric to be stitched is stuck to the revealed stabilizer and the embroidery is worked. ▲

Soluble stabilizers
These range from webs and soft-handle fabrics that look like interfacings to clear films available in different thicknesses. The weight and thickness of the stabilizer will determine how easy it is to wash away. Some of the light web-like stabilizers will disintegrate when sprayed with water, while heavier films need repeated soaking. Heat-away versions are dissolved by pressing with a hot iron. ▼

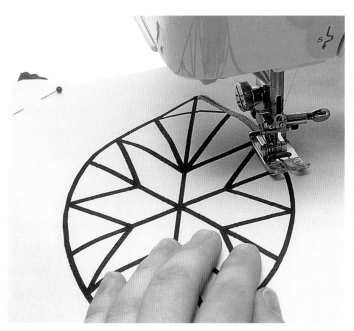

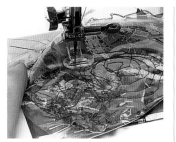

Paper solubles can be printed on—thus, stitch designs can be created on a computer and printed onto the stabilizer. The design is then embroidered through the stabilizer onto the fabric. Once finished, the stabilizer is washed away. ▲

Lightweight film and web stabilizers are ideal for delicate fabrics or can be used at the back and front of pile fabrics to provide stability and prevent the embroidery stitching disappearing into the fabric pile. Again, once stitched, the stabilizers are washed away. ▼

Heavyweight film stabilizer is ideal for creating stitched sculptures. It is advisable to use a darning foot and embroidery hoop, although not absolutely necessary as the film is heavy and stable. A design can be drawn onto the film before being stitched through onto the fabric. Alternatively, simply stitch all over the film in a pattern or randomly, making sure that all stitches are joined, adding thread and fabric scraps, etc. for texture. ▲

Dissolve the stabilizer completely to leave a lacy fabric. Also dissolve partially and then dry over a shape such as a bowl or glass, to create a thread sculpture. ▲

Heat-away stabilizer Ideal when it is impossible to wash the fabric. It is removed by placing a hot dry iron (cotton setting) on the stabilizer until it turns brown (10–15 seconds). The resulting dust is then brushed away with a soft-bristle brush. For delicate fabrics, use a cooler temperature for slightly longer. ▼

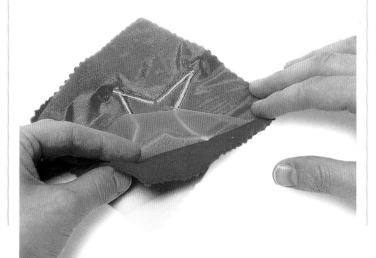

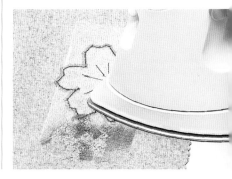

Cutwork

Like many specialist creative-sewing techniques, cutwork was traditionally done by hand, taking many painstaking hours to cut and stitch in order to create lacy designs for table linen, etc. Nowadays, a basic sewing machine with straight and zigzag stitches can be used to create the same finish in minutes rather than months.

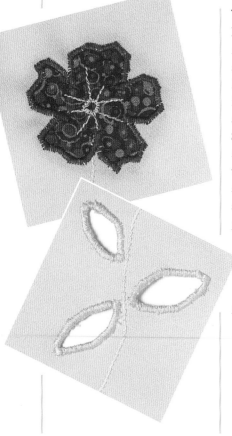

THE BASICS

Fabric Ideal fabrics are medium-weight, woven fabrics such as cotton, linen, or linen-like blends. Avoid soft limp fabrics that will not stay stable after cutting.

Stabilizers A lightweight soluble stabilizer and medium-weight or paper-soluble stabilizer. Use the lightweight stabilizer to stitch a design in place and the paper stabilizer to hold the cut area of the fabric in place for final stitching.

Needle Use a size 12 (80) machine needle.

STEPS TO SEW

1 Trace the chosen design onto one layer of lightweight, soluble stabilizer using a vanishing marking pen, then pin the stabilizer to the right side of the fabric, with the design facing up.

2 Using a straight stitch and stitch length of 1.5, sew around the design outline. ▶

> **TIP** *Always test a sample stitch length on the same combination of layers before stitching the project.*

3 Stitch around the design again, this time using a small zigzag stitch. ▼

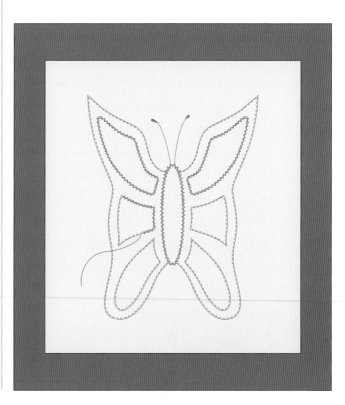

4 Cut the middle of the design out using a pair of sharp embroidery scissors. Avoid cutting the stitching but if you do, over stitch immediately. Press. ▼

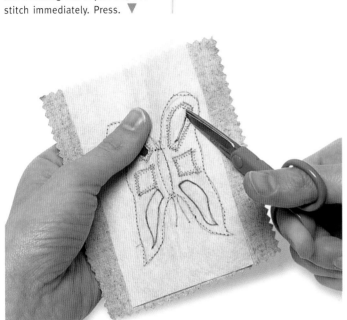

5 Pin and baste a layer of medium-weight or paper stabilizer to the back of the fabric, large enough to cover the cutwork area. This helps feed the fabric evenly through the feed dogs for the final stitching.

6 Adjust the zigzag stitch to a satin stitch (length of 0.4 and width 3.5) and stitch again all over the existing stitching. The right swing of the needle should be stitching just on the stabilizer in order to seal/encase the cut edges completely.

7 Wash the cutwork to dissolve the stabilizers and allow to dry before pressing again with a dry iron.

SHADOW CUTWORK

Shadow cut work is similar, but the cut-out areas are backed by a contrasting (usually transparent) fabric. Work steps 1–2 as above, then:

3 Carefully cut the middle of the design out using a pair of sharp embroidery scissors.

TIP *When working cutwork areas, use fabrics that do not unravel easily.*

4 Pin and baste the contrasting fabric behind the design area, making sure there is sufficient to cover the complete cutwork area.

5 Stitch around the design as step 3 above, using a small zigzag stitch and satin stitch. ▲

6 Completely cover the cut edges of the top layer of fabric. Once covered, dissolve any remaining stabilizer and press as before. ▼

TIP *Use different shades of contrasting fabrics to create an interesting effect.*

GALLERY

So much can be achieved using a few basic stitches, a sewing machine, and lots of imagination. Whether you wish to make clothes for yourself or your family, redecorate with new soft furnishings, or just get really creative, we have a gallery of work to inspire you.

JENNIE RAYMENT, *known internationally for her "twiddling and fiddling" fabric manipulation, stitches, clips, folds, and tucks fabrics into unusual shapes, which she then incorporates into everyday items.*

ABOVE **Trumpets!** For this design Jennie has tucked and folded squares of fabric, catch stitching the folds in place before quilting them onto a cushion front. The work is machine stitched and finished with free-motion quilting.

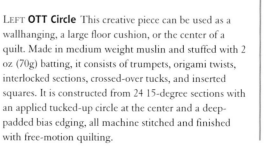

LEFT **OTT Circle** This creative piece can be used as a wallhanging, a large floor cushion, or the center of a quilt. Made in medium weight muslin and stuffed with 2 oz (70g) batting, it consists of trumpets, origami twists, interlocked sections, crossed-over tucks, and inserted squares. It is constructed from 24 15-degree sections with an applied tucked-up circle at the center and a deep-padded bias edging, all machine stitched and finished with free-motion quilting.

ABOVE **Table Triumph!** These perky placements were made for *Sewing World* magazine, for which Jennie is a regular contributor. There are no curved seams—again, she used her folding and tucking technique to create a masterly illusion.

FREUDENBERG (VILENE, PELLON) *have been making interfacings for many years and continue to develop new products for today's increasingly creative sewers.*

RIGHT **Fashioned Fabric**
By using one of the new soluble web products, very individual fabrics can be made. Strips of threads, ribbons, yarns, and fabric scraps were sandwiched between two layers of soluble stabilizer and then stitched all over in straight lines, swirls, zigzags, etc. Once the layers were covered in stitching, the stabilizers were washed away to leave the newly fashioned fabric—ideal for scarves, hats, vests, or pillow covers.

BRITISH TRIMMINGS, *part of the Conso Group, are well known for their glorious range of trimmings.*

LEFT **Red Corner** Simple pillow shapes are easy to make and yet, with trims added, become very individual and can be made to perfectly match your décor. Buying similarly trimmed pillows in stores would be very expensive!

CHRISTINE PORTER *is a well-known quilter and designer who teaches and writes on the subject. She loves collecting fabrics of all kinds and finds inspiration in the different combinations and colors, as well as in floor tiles!*

RIGHT **Stripey hugs and kisses** This designed was inspired by the floor tiles of a chemist shop in Ambleside, England. The design detail is picked out by the bold horizontal and vertical grid, while a touch of black for the triangles emphasizes the crosses of brilliant yellow and the black-and-white star fabric adds an extra twist in the red centers. The design was quilted by Jenny Spencer on a long-arm machine.

GILDA BARON *is a textile artist famous for her creative landscapes.*

BELOW **Moonlight** This was inspired by after-dinner walks, while in Scotland. For the background, Gilda used batik—a hot wax resist. Over this, she applied machine and hand embroidery and then completed the picture with applied pieces of hand-dyed fabric.

LEFT **Purple prose** The basis of inspiration for this quilt is an entrance hall in a gentlemen's club! The placement of the dark colors gives the illusion of curved piecing but in fact they all have straight lines. The piece combines purples with turquoise, emphasizing the design from corner to corner. By extending the dark central triangles into the center of the borders, Christine created a frame and focus for the design. Quilted by Beryl Cadman.

ABOVE **The Moody Loch** The moody colors of a rainy day by the loch inspired Gilda to make this piece of work. Batik was used to create the background. This was then machined, hand stitched, and some hand-dyed pieces of fabric applied. The work then went back to the machine to be stitched onto handmade paper. More hand and machine stitch was applied and it was completed with birds painted onto the paper.

ABOVE **Poppies** This miniature is one of a set of hand-made greetings cards. The background was hand-dyed; the poppies were then drawn by fabric pen and machine embroidered over the top using free-motion embroidery.

RIGHT **Waving grasses** Another greetings card inspired by the natural world. Pieces of metallic wrapping paper were pasted onto the paper and then machine embroidered over the top. The piece was turned sideways to machine the grasses and then turned back the right way to create the flowers with a zigzag stitch.

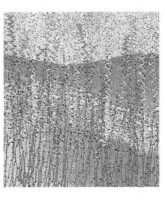

ABOVE **Moorland at dawn** Subtle, muted colors give an almost Impressionistic feel to this piece. The background was hand-dyed with broad swathes of color. The detail of the grasses was created by free-motion embroidery. Metallic threads bring out the glinting highlights in the foreground. The shapes of the birds were added with a gold highlighter pen.

LESLEY GEORGE *is a designer and creative textile artist. She has a studio in Hampshire, England from which she teaches and works to commission.*

ABOVE AND RIGHT Butterfly brooch This piece's lace-effect free-machine embroidery was made on acetate dissolved in acetone.

RIGHT **Organism** This is a top made for Lesley's daughter from dyed and foiled silk velvet. The neckline is appliquéd with foiled and burned synthetic velvets, and embellished with "stocking stuff" (stitching into stockings). The edges are machine satin stitched. This garment has been hand finished with beads and sequins. Most of the machine stitching has been done with metallic embroidery threads.

LEFT AND BELOW RIGHT **Midsummer Night's Dream bridal** The inspiration for this bridal gown and accessories came from a number of sources. The original idea was to make the bodice out of scraps of fabrics left from other wedding gowns. As Lesley had been developing her skills working with soluble fabrics to make lace effects, she decided to incorporate this technique. The design for the lace was inspired by the organic forms of Art Nouveau. It has developed into something very Ice Queen-like, although it could be a dress for Titania, hence the name.

For the boned bodice, silks and metallics were stitched to a background fabric to create texture. This was lined in heavy silk habutai. The bodice is edged with lace-effect machine embroidery worked on cold water-soluble fabric, while the back bodice is laced with machine-wrapped cord finished with tassels. The neckline is also finished with twisted, machine-wrapped cord. The detachable sleeves are silk chiffon with insets of machine-embroidered lace effects reinforced with silk tulle. The skirt is cut on the cross in double silk crepe lined in silk habutai, finished at the hem with pale gold metallic thread. The choker is also lace effects worked on cold water-soluble fabric, embellished with beads. The tiara was made with the acetate and acetone technique for the lace, with wired beads, and a machine-wrapped wire base.

CLAIRE SHAEFFER *has been a designer and writer for many years. Her particular specialty is working with and sharing couture techniques, thus providing home dressmakers with the ability to achieve superb results.*

BELOW **Red dress** Designed by Claire for Vogue Patterns, Costume Couture Collection, this dress has lots of couture details, now available to home dressmakers. It is Vogue Pattern 7540, sizes 6–22.

ABOVE AND RIGHT **Lined coat** Another design by Claire for Vogue Patterns, Costume Couture Collection, the instructions provided include full couture techniques or simpler dressmaking techniques. It is Vogue Pattern 7634, sizes 6–22.

LEFT **Pleated trousers** This is a classic trouser design, created by Claire for Vogue Patterns, Costume Couture Collection. The front pleats provide a flattering finish to the waist, emphasized by the straight leg. Vogue Pattern 7468, sizes 6–22.

WENDY GARDINER,

*author, has created projects,
written books, and edited
magazines for over 20 years.*

ABOVE, RIGHT AND BELOW
Curtains and pillows Adding trims
to plain drapes and pillows has
turned these simple soft furnishings
into a luxurious boudoir setting.
The trims have been stitched in-
seam along the edges of drapes,
voiles, and bed valance, and top
stitched to the pillows.

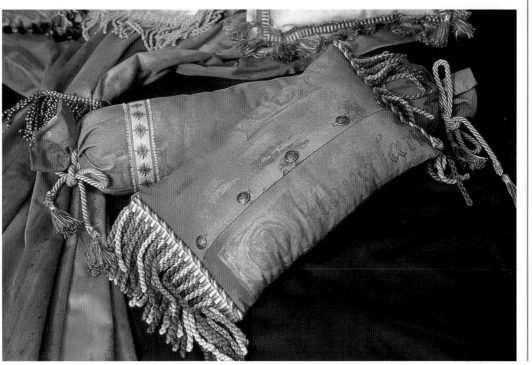

ABOVE **Cream blouse** Made in a
plain linen-look fabric, this classic
blouse design provides a wardrobe
staple that transcends the
changing seasons.

ABOVE Embroidered elegance
The exquisite embroidery on this silk chiffon needed only the simplest of dirndl skirt designs. Gathered at the waist and lined with matching silk, the embroidery border takes full glory.

LEFT Blush pink bags These two totes by Betty Barnden are easy to make, combining straight stitching with a selection of funky trims top-stitched in place.

JANET MOVILLE *has been teaching couture sewing techniques for many years and loves to share her knowledge and techniques.*

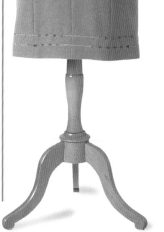

LEFT AND BELOW **Mother of the Bride** A Vogue pattern Bill Blass designer jacket in lilac-plaid Linton tweed is an effective match with the tailored cap-sleeve sheath dress with simple, effective detail at the neckline and hem. Specialty yarn drawn from the jacket fabric was couched into place on the dress. The matching bag was made as an insert to a Suzy Smith transparent design, to complete the ensemble.

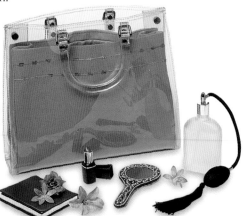

ABOVE AND BELOW **Wedding dress** Miniscule piping is applied to every conceivable seam of this bodice. Pure silk duchesse satin is overlaid with silk-embroidered chiffon. The back has mock lacing on the bodice with lavish embroidery and hand beading on the back panel of the skirt.

ALISON SMITH *runs a sewing studio and teaches at a number of sewing-machine centers.*

RIGHT **Butterfly jacket** This exquisitely embroidered jacket and skirt is made in 100% silk. The jacket is covered in embroidery that was done on the Janome Memory Craft 10000 sewing machine featuring designs from the 9000 and 10000 sewing machines. The embroidery was executed prior to the jacket being constructed. After construction rhinestones were added to the embroidery. A straight skirt completes the outfit.

LEFT **Classic jacket** This is a classic jacket featuring revers and welt pockets with a flap. The jacket is made from a lilac Linton fabric with a multicolored thread running through it. Whilst the lilac fabric is a wool crêpe yarn, the multicolored yarn has is non-woven and forms small loops on the surface.

LORNA KNIGHT *is particularly well known for her lingerie and serger sewing.*

BELOW **Cream and gold soft-stretch lace nightdress** This very simple garment was made almost entirely on a four-thread overlocker. The top edge was finished with a band cut from the same fabric, taking advantage of its Lycra™ stretch properties. Lorna used the quarter pinning method, to overlock it in place and to finish the hem. Straps were sewn and applied with a conventional sewing machine.

ABOVE **Antique white cotton lawn camisole top and shorts**
Camisole Cut on the bias, the front panel was created using a twin needle and a decorative machine stitch. The panel was faced with the cotton lawn, then sewn to the center front and the side fronts before being sewn to the back. The top edge was finished with a bias-cut strip. The narrow straps have the same decorative machine stitch to reflect the front panel, and were sewn in with the bias strip, which anchors and conceals the raw edges.
Shorts Also finished with a twin needle and decorative machine stitch detail at the hem, quarter pinning was used to apply the lightweight elastic to the waist giving a soft, comfortable finish.

SUE HAZELL *runs her own studio, teaching soft furnishings, as well as running women's groups on a national level.*

LEFT **Co-ordinating pillows** A self-flanged border with contrasting top stitching has been used to complement the contrast insert. These are straightforward to make by cutting two squares of each fabric and machining contrast fabric to the main fabric all around to create two pieces. Cut a slit on the contrast side only, across the center but less than the pad size. Turn and press, sandwich together, and top stitch on three sides. Finish by pushing a pad into the gap and then slip stitching the gap closed.

ABOVE **Roman blind** Featured in our Soft Furnishing section, a Roman blind uses only enough fabric to cover the area required plus a small amount for turnings, therefore a small remnant of a costly fabric can be used to create an expensive-looking window treatment. These blinds also work well in a vertical-striped fabric.

JANE BENNETT *is first and foremost a graphic artist, but one who loves to sew creatively.*

RIGHT **Trinket boxes** Jane made these exquisite boxes for friends using a combination of machine embroidery and hand sewing. Each also has little secret drawers with movable shelves inside. The embroidery designs were first downloaded from the internet and then customized to suit each box.

BETTY BARNDEN *has written a number of books and is a regular contributor to a range of titles including* Sewing World *magazine.*

BELOW **Capture the garden** For this wall hanging, Betty took a picture when her garden was in bloom and then used a transfer paper to transfer the image to fabric. Once transferred, Betty used a combination of straight stitching and free-motion embroidery to stitch over the image.

ABOVE **Souffle bag** A simple design, made special with the couched silver-thread design. To continue the color scheme, Betty added a silver lining and silver cord ties.

RIGHT **Metallic magic** Betty used a soluble stabilizer to create these metallic thread bowls. Once the design is stitched, the stabilizer is washed away, leaving just the thread stitching. To form the shape, Betty pressed the damp stitching over a glass and a bowl to form their shape. Once dry, the bowls retain their shape.

JOAN GORDON *has designed and created craft projects for a number of magazines internationally.*

BELOW **Cutwork blouse** Cutwork was traditionally done by hand to embellish tablecloths and fine linen, but today, with a few innovative haberdashery products, cutwork can be made on a basic sewing machine. Here the cutwork was created before the blouse was made up. Ideal fabrics are medium-weight cotton, linen, and linen blends.

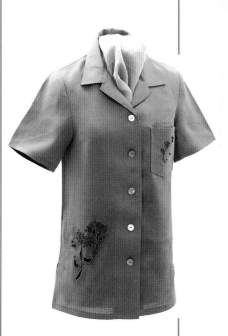

Reference charts

NEEDLE TYPES ▼ ▶

Choose the appropriate needle for each fabric type. The weight of fabric, number of layers, and stitch density determine the needle size.

Hand stitching needle types

Needle type	Fabric
UNIVERSAL/MULTIPURPOSE	Woven fabrics, synthetics, knits. Good general purpose needle.
BALL POINT	Knits, double knits, fleece, stretch, ribbing, fake furs.
STRETCH	Two-way stretch fabrics, lingerie, swimwear, Lycra™, elastic.
JEANS	Heavyweight cottons, canvas, denim, tightly woven fabrics, faux suede, faux leathers
SHARPS/MICROFIBER	Silks, satins, voiles, fine fabrics, polyesters, microfiber fabrics.
LEATHER	Leather, suede, plastic.
EMBROIDERY	Machine embroidery, sewing specialty or metallic threads.
QUILTING	Multi-layer, patchwork/quilting work.
TWIN	Works two rows of parallel stitching at same time. Use needle size appropriate for fabric.

FABRIC CONVERSION CHART ▶

Use the Fabric width conversion chart to determine the amount of fabric required when the chosen material differs in width to that listed on the pattern envelope.

TIP *Unusual patterns, one-way designs, and with-nap fabrics may effect the amount needed—check with your fabric retailer.*

Calculation method

If a pattern calls for 2 yards of 36 in wide fabric (1.85m of 90cm), and your chosen fabric is 45 in (115cm) wide, look along the column from the 2 yards under 36 in wide to the 45 in column. The amount of fabric required at the different width is noted here (1⅝ yd or 1.5m).

Hand stitching needle Types

Needle sizes

American	European	Fabric weight
9	60	fine, lightweight, chiffon, voiles
10	70	lightweight, organza, silks
11	75	lingerie, swimwear, fine cottons
12	80	general dressmaking—cottons, lightweight woolens, polyesters, velvets
14	90	heavier weight woolens, wool crepes, coatings,fleece, soft furnishing cottons
16	100	heavyweight coatings, dense denim, canvas, heavy brocade, etc.
18	110	heavyweight fabrics, multi-layers, soft furnishing
20	120	very heavyweight

Fabric width conversion chart

36 in. YARDS	90 cm METERS	45 in. YARDS	115 cm METERS	54 in. YARDS	140 cm METERS	60 in. YARDS	150 cm METERS
1¾	1.60	1⅜	1.30	1⅛	1.05	1	0.95
2	1.85	1⅝	1.50	1⅜	1.30	1¼	1.15
2¼	2.10	1¾	1.60	1½	1.50	1⅜	1.30
2½	2.30	2⅛	1.95	1¾	1.60	1⅝	1.50
2⅞	2.65	2¼	2.10	1⅞	1.75	1¾	1.60
3⅛	2.90	2½	2.30	2	1.85	1⅞	1.75
3⅜	3.10	2¾	2.55	2¼	2.10	2	1.85
3¾	3.45	2⅞	2.65	2⅜	2.20	2¼	2.10
4¼	3.90	3⅛	2.90	2⅝	2.40	2⅜	2.20
4½	4.15	3⅜	3.10	2¾	2.55	2⅝	2.40
4¾	4.35	3⅝	3.35	2⅞	2.65	2¾	2.55
5	4.60	3⅞	3.55	3⅛	2.90	2⅞	2. 65

Web resource guide

There are many interesting and useful sites on the internet. We have picked a few sources for patterns, fabrics, online learning, and pattern design software.

SEWING MACHINE COMPANIES

The following sites provide information on their latest sewing machines and sergers (overlockers). Some also have sewing tips, free projects, and stockist information.

www.babylock.com OR babylock.co.uk (for UK visitors)

www.berninausa.com OR bernina.co.uk (for UK visitors)

www.brother.com OR brother.co.uk (for UK visitors)

www.husqvarnaviking.com

www.janome.com

www.pfaff.com

www.singer.com

PATTERN DESIGN SOFTWARE

www.wildginger.com
Find information and stockist details for Patternmaster Boutique, Child's Play and Tailor Made. Use personal measurements to create a variety of garments in mix and match designs.

www.livingsoft.com
All three Dressshop versions are available to purchase online at this website. For more details and for advice on choosing the correct package, pay them a visit.

www.softbyte.com
Make personalized patterns on your PC using Fittingly Sew. Input measurements into basic block patterns, then use the drawing tools to create the required style. Buy the software directly from this site.

www.cadterns.com
Basic block patterns and a "cyber school" are available from this site. You'll also find information about pattern drafting using computer assisted pattern makers.

PATTERN COMPANIES

Some of the commercial pattern companies will sell patterns via mail order. For others, the sites provide the opportunity of viewing all the available designs before purchasing from retailers. These are all international sites with pages for the different countries.

www.kwiksew.com
This site provides a list of mail order dealers.

www.simplicity.com
Shows all current designs for Simplicity and New Look patterns. Also offers specialist catalogs for home use.

www.voguepatterns.com
The complete collections from McCalls, Butterick, and Vogue patterns.

www.marfy.it
An elegant and sophisticated range of Italian patterns with a list of international retailers.

www.thesewingplace.com
A lovely selection from independent designers.

PATTERNS AND FABRICS

Again, the following sites offer mail order for fabrics and patterns.

www.sewingstudio.com
This site is overflowing with a superb selection of fabrics, including winter, family, fashion. All available to buy online.

www.sawyerbrook.com
Another fantastic fabric site that offers seasonal fabrics, fashion, and a wonderful discount section. There is also a fabulous selection of buttons available.

www.patternshowcase.com
A great site for patterns from all the major pattern companies, including Kwik Sew, New Look, Vogue, Butterick, Simplicity, and McCalls. Patterns are also available to buy online from less well-known designers such as Ragstock, Folkwear, and Encore.

www.sewingpatterns.com
This site has a huge selection of patterns that can be ordered online. Choose from Simplicity, New Look, Vogue, Kwik Sew, and McCalls, plus some less well-known brands and browse the catalogues at leisure.

Index

Credits

The author would like to extend special thanks to Makower Fabrics for fabrics used throughout the book, to Simplicity and Janome for the loan of their sewing machines, to Gütermann for thread, and Vilene (Pellon) for interfacing.

Quarto would like to thank the following for supplying pictures reproduced in this book:

(Key: l=left, r=right, c=center, t=top, b=bottom)

Vogue Patterns
p2, p25c, p96l;
tel:+44 (0)870 777 9966
www.sewdirect.com

Crowson Fabrics
p 92;
tel:+44 (0)207 823 3294
www.crowsonfabrics.com

Rufflette Ltd
p92tl, p94 all pictures;
tel: +44 (0)161 998 1811,
www.rufflette.com

Attitude Photography
p146, p147, p149, p154b, p155t;
tel:+44 (0)23 92 261338

All other photographs and illustrations are the copyright of Quarto Publishing plc.

While every effort has been made to credit contributors, Quarto would like to apologize should there have been any omissions or errors.

Contacts

USA

Makower Fabrics
1359 Broadway
New York
NY 10018
www.concordfabrics.com

Simplicity Pattern Co Inc (USA)
Distributors of Simplicity, New Look and Burda patterns
2 Park Avenue, 12th Floor
New York
NY 10016
www.simplicity.com

McCalls Pattern Company (USA)
11 Penn Plaza
New York
NY 10001
www.maccall.com

Kwik Sew Pattern Company Inc (USA)
3000 Washington Avenue North
Minneapolis
NM 55411-1699
www.kwiksew.com

Pellon Freudenberg Non Wovens
3440 Industrial Drive
Durham
NC 27704
www.www.vilene.com

Gütermann of America Inc
8227 Arrowridge Blvd
Charlotte
NC 28273
www.gutermann.com

Conso Group (USA)
PO Box 326
513 North Duncan Bypass
Union
SC 29379
www.conso.com

Coats and Clark (USA)
4135 South Stream Blvd
Charlotte
NC 28217

Textol Systems Inc (Rufflette USA)
435 Meadow Lane
Carlstadt
NJ 07675
www.textol.com

Janome Sewing Machines
10 Industrial Ave
Mahwah
NJ 07430
www.janome.com

UK

Simplicity Ltd (UK)
PO Box 367
Coronation Street
Stockport
Cheshire
SK5 7W2
www.simplicity.com

Makower Fabrics UK
118 Greys Road
Henley on Thames,
Oxon
RG9 1QW
www.makoweruk.com

Perival Gütermann
Bullsbrook Road
Hayes
Middx
UB4 OJR
www.gutermann.com

McCalls, Butterick and Vogue Patterns (UK)
New Lane
Havant
Hants
PO9 2ND
www.maccall.com

Kwik Sew (UK)
c/o Elna Sewing Machines
B2 Lanterns Court
Millharbour
London
E14 9TU
www.kwiksew.com

Vilene Retail (Freudenberg)
Lowfields Business Park
Elland
West Yorkshire
HX5 5DX
www.vilene.com

Rufflette Ltd (UK)
Sharston Road
Manchester
M22 4TH
www.rufflette.com

British Trimmings (UK)
PO Box 46
Coronation Street
Stockport
Cheshire
SK5 7PJ
www.britishtrimmings.co.uk

Coats Crafts UK Ltd
(Also distributors of Prym products)
PO Box 22
The Lingfield Estate
McMullen Road
Darlington
DL1 1YQ
www.coatscrafts.co.uk

Janome Sewing Machines
Janome Centre
Southside
Cheshire
SK6 2SP
www.janome.co.uk